To Helen
your never
too old.
Ian.

I could not have achieved the completion of this book without the vast help and thoughtful guidance, from a whole range of people. Firstly the people who gave me my life, love and have now passed over my Parents and Grandmother, Siblings and all the many experiences they have given me, good or bad, throughout my years before this book was even born.

Also I would like to thank my children. Had it not been for you both then I don't think I would have survived throughout these years of change. I also thank all my extended and related family over the years, for putting up with my agonising behaviour, some of which was helpful and some which was definitely not.
Individually I would like to thank the following for being there and helping me to understand the counselling world and all its complexities.

>Sue: for giving me the energy and total support to carry on.
>Neil: for being there and my constant supportive guide.
>Faye: for putting the words from hours of audio onto paper.
>My clients: who I have learnt so much from.
>Pam: sadly not with us any more, for making me believe in me.

>My tutors: along the way, official and unofficial.

And the customary anyone who knows me and has helped me along my path of discovery, too many to mention, but you know who you are,
This is for you.
- Disclaimer: The guidance, advice, and suggested tools contained within this book are for inspirational purposes only. No opinions are implied as the only way to look at the world or indeed interact with it with regard to relational health, wellbeing or the causes of mental ill health. The information contained within this book is in no way intended to diagnose or replace professional care and attention that you may wish to seek. If you feel you have a relational condition of any nature that requires a consultation, examination or indeed medication, you are encouraged to consult another appropriate professional.

Why should I buy this book?

This Book or journey is a self-help guide based on over 8,000 hours of counselling practice and the many years of helping myself, and countless Individuals, Couples and Families with their issues and to obtain quality healthy relationships. It will help you to understand why people act the way they do and in doing so will help you to solve the problems that we have and then to have better relationships with anyone that you interact with or you are connected to. That could be Colleagues, Friends, Family, or loved ones.

Unless you live on a dessert island, and don't interact with other humans, this book will help you to have the life you want instead of the one other people think you should have. Buy the book and escape the restrictions in your life.

It is intended as a helpful aid, but your life is still your life, you need to make decisions and take responsibility for you own actions. These techniques and thoughts are tried and tested; I hope they will help you as much as they have helped me and the countless people I have helped over the years.

If you find anything which is not grammatically correct or spelt right then I apologise but I wanted this to be as authentic as it possibly could be to be ME even the dyslexic me.

"Have the life you want not the one other people think you should have"

Additions to my work and further input can be found at
www.seekingchange.co.uk
If you feel that you would like to interact with my professional training courses then please feel free to contact me through
www.intuitivetherapy.co.uk
Text Copyright ©2011 Ian Wallace
All Rights Reserved

Table of Contents

Chapter 1
The initial Journey
Chapter 2
Finding myself and were I fitted
Chapter 3
Something I am finally good at
Chapter 4
Communication
Chapter 5
Working from historical scripts
Chapter 6
Breaking chains that bind us to the past
Chapter 7
The dynamics of Humans
Chapter 8
Systems and Surviving Them
Chapter 9
A Better Understanding of Interactions with Others
Control and Insecurity
Chapter 10
Intuitive processes
Chapter 11
In the Now

Chapter 12
What and Why
Onwards

Tools   from page 168
Time Out
Script Awareness tool
Loss Cycle
Telling not Asking
No One is an Island
Re-evaluating process
Are you in charge of your life?
Power Wall to enhance change
Fears and challenging them
Using fear constructively
Using alternative words
Cycle of Insecure Talking
Pebble in the pond process
Win Win process
Challenging Life Scripts
Identifying and Changing Scripts
Co-Dependency
The level of masks we show

Perception and reality

Systems and how they interconnect

Talking Time

Working with Affairs

Quality Time

Working with Grief

The Way Forward to Seeking Change

Letters to release un-processed Emotions

The Route away from Depression

Why people use put downs and ways to stop it

Using symbolism instead of words to communicate our feelings

Offerings not Statements

Time together and apart, getting the right balance, for a healthy relationship

Is your Relationship in need of help?

Process to change

Using deflective behaviours

Immediacy

Having hard conversations

You will find throughout this book the following pointers. These awareness areas are split into different ways of helping you, look for these symbols and they will give you an understanding of the type of awareness I am looking to input for you.

Light bulb moments, (when a realisation had occurred for me)

Tools to fix things, (more explanation about the tool can be found in the tool box section at the end of the book)

Things for you to think about (these sections helps to give you more awareness and enables ways to enhance and increase your understanding of you and the reasons that you interact the way you do)

Chapter 1
The initial Journey

The beginning of the journey, which I do believe, is a journey, albeit based on my individual journey, is one that, as with most of life's journeys, the start is never really a realisation that this was a journey, that is to say it's just an coincidental occurrence or a singular situation or scenario that sets the ball rolling in some sense there is never, in my opinion, something that is not connected to another thing all of our life is one big journey. Individually I suppose for me it was in the moving from a position of security being married, having a family, doing everything I thought I should do in order to make everything work and everything happen. Getting stuck in the old rut of what I now know to be life scripts.

Life scripts are the things that we are taught, told, or shown, when we are children and as we grow up, by our significant others, whether that's parents, grandparents, peer groups or indeed whoever we have trust in really. They can be good scripts or not so good scripts for us.

Know your life scripts and you know yourself. What do you think your life scripts are and how do they control your life, are they good or bad for you?

Use the script awareness tool in order to find your scripts and track them to see if they are helpful or not.

One of my life scripts was, coming down through my Dad, that you worked and worked and that you are selfish and everything else happens because your wife does whatever else was needed to be done. That's a very old fashioned way of looking at things, which it is.
I now know this to be the wrong way for me to do things. At that time in my life it was just a case of getting stuck in the rut of that life script and working harder and longer hours to bring in whatever income I needed in order to make it work, my Wife's life and my Family's life was a secondary drive. My Wife, at that time, just thought I did not want to be with her or the family, understandably so given that I was never fully cognitively there or even at home most weeks.

In this process I found I had disengaged from the relationship with my then Wife and with the family.

Over a period of time, like a lot of relationships which are in difficulty, that I am now aware of and see in my counselling rooms, we grew apart; losing the couple connection between us and then also losing whatever it is that joins two people together in the first place.
Understandably then our relationship was no more, and what is it the relationship? It's there only to be Mum and Dad, parents and I suppose that's what I went through, in a sense, without realising it.
That's not to say I don't take away any responsibility that I have in that process of deterioration, I do. I made choices, even if I didn't necessarily know which choices I was making. You cannot blame the people who give us our life scripts you have to take the responsibility to choose whether to follow them or not. It is their message but your life.

Even if you sit on the fence you are making a choice to do so. Taking ownership of any situation is a great way to help the process of moving forward, by taking responsibility you take control and by taking control you steer your future path.

13

Blaming does not help you or them as blaming just gets you stuck in the past.

I suppose my world, or the world I knew, changed when that relationship fell apart and my sense of what was happening to me were opened my wider understanding of the world. During the time of my significant re-adjustment and a total rearrangement of the secure life I thought I had. Previously my view of our future was that we would grow old together, retire, and have a little cottage by the sea. The fairy tale kind of thought process, which I suppose a lot of people have.

One day it, the dream, was no more and I found myself in a strange world of uncertainty, lost and in a limbo land, floating it seemed on an iceberg not knowing where I might end up, out of control and drifting with the tide of uncertainty.

The loss cycle of change is a strange world to be in; it didn't seem to have any structure to it. I went from being in total control of my life, or so I thought, what an idiot I was to not realise that I was completely out of control.

Thinking you can ever be in control of life is absurd, you can only be aware and in charge of the time you are in. At this moment I am typing something the next thought may be different I can only type one letter at a time so I am in control of that letter, not the sentence that follows. Otherwise I would not miss-spell anything and I frequently do. I would never be wrong and I frequently am.

Take a moment and see what you are really in control of, scary isn't it?

I don't now blame anybody for that change; I accept it was my fault. I did unfortunately blame others at the time of that change; I wanted to blame anyone and everyone. I could not accept the responsibility of the process at the time. It is only with the passing of time and some healing that I came to this understanding.

Whilst I was stuck in that blaming world I did many things that I truly regret and I am sorry to the people who were around me at that time, my previous Wife, Children, Friends and Relationships as I know I did not treat you well and with the respect you deserved.

I also say Sorry to myself as I also know that the person I was at that time was not the real me that I have come to find now. I hurt myself as well as others thinking I did not deserve to live, that others would be better off without me in their life. Being so full of contempt for myself and guilt of what I had or had not done.

I bless the moment when I realised the silliness of the thoughts I was having and the fact that the transportation I had sought to take me from this world never materialised. I now realise it was just that we weren't really in a relationship, in the true sense of the word, so I fully understand now why those things happened, and that was a reason for making this journey, trying to inform myself more about why things had happened, why relationships don't work and now trying to help other people not to get to that point, in order to help them to move into a different or better place or space in their relationships.

Journeying through that process, finding the readjustment of this my new life, losing the old relationship, waking up from being in that numbing limbo land, in one depressive sense. I went through about 2 – 21/2 years of re-adjustment, re-awareness, re-thinking, re-organisation, and just lots of other re's in between.

I came to the conclusion that the journey that I had taken, through that part of my life, was one where, in some senses I lost myself……. and then thankfully found myself again. A new and definitely different me or maybe just the real me, that had never been shown to or understood by the outside world including myself.

For anyone who has been through that process, it can be a harrowing and soul destroying experience and also strangely quite an invigorating one at the same time. I did a lot of things that were ok and I did a lot of things that probably weren't ok. Through a sheer terrifying, trying to find me liberating process. I fumbled my way through that time and thankfully came out the other side into a place where I could evaluate my position. I thought "What do I want to do, where do I want to go? What is going to be my life now? How do I earn money? Who do I earn money for?" All forward thinking processes future possibilities, which makes you realise that you're through the depression and loss part of the process and then I came to a conclusion that I had to also re-evaluate my skills and abilities.

When you can start to think about the future you are really coming through the loss and depression cycle and starting to begin the process of future change.

Previous to that I'd always been in 'people' jobs, people connective trades, Retail, Sales and training roles.
I had always been good at talking to people and considered myself a pretty good people orientated person, which is strange really considering I could not connect to the person that was closest to me at that time. I think she found me controlling and not able to listen it's a communication issue that I call Telling not Asking due to insecurities.

Telling not asking

I've found that with the couples I see, they can be really good communicators in their chosen fields but cannot communicate effectively within the relationships they have.
I now understand why this is so, as there is far too much to lose in our closest relationships, so we are basically insecure in those relationships. This makes us test those relationships with our communication and starts a process of trying to see if the relationship is as safe and secure as we would like it to be.

This could be possibly result in finishing off other people's sentences, saying what we believe they are thinking or feeling, creating arguments over silly insignificant things.

This insecurity makes us react in a non-objective way, not being able to see what we are doing, taking us down a path on non-communication or non-effective communication.

Re-evaluating process; will give you clearness of thoughts and steer through the muddy paths of future options, clearing away your doubts and your uncertainty helping you to see what it is that you want for your future.

So I started re-evaluating what it was that I really wanted out of my life. I really wanted to stop being in the rat race, as it was affectionately called in those days, and possibly still is, although being out of it over now for the last 18 years I'm not sure I am qualified to comment. I needed to stop having the competitiveness of being in a sales orientated profession and try to find something that I felt comfortable with, that I was hopefully good at and one in which I could be my own person my own boss, whilst still helping people. This I found very scary but also an invigorating, exciting and experiential kind of thought process. As I'd always clicked with people in my work and been around people and talking to people, that seemed to be the best thing to try and look at.

Also the fact that I'd been through a relationship breakdown and I was becoming fascinated with why people do what people do and their interactions with others also being fascinated with human relationships in general.

With the personal experiences over that 2 – 21/2 years (readjustment period) of losing myself and finding myself, I had picked up a lot of awareness and understanding of myself and the process I had been through, seeing things in a different way, coming from a different perspective. Not seeing the glass as half empty anymore but instead as half full. That was something that had happened to me over that period and I had gained immense strength from it.

The tools I'd acquired, honed and used to survive throughout that process, and sometimes it was definitely a survival process, I thought that maybe I could use them to help other people who were trying to come to terms with life's changes.

In my life there have been moments, as probably most people have in their lives, of what we class as synchronicity or coincidence or whatever you would like to call it.
I think for me I can give you an important example of a small insignificant detail which shows it perfectly and resonates with a specific day in the late part of 1999.

I was walking through Leeds Rail station in City Square and some marketing people were outside the station entrance, as they sometimes are, handing out copies of the Yorkshire Evening Post. I didn't normally buy a paper as I'm not necessarily a reading kind of person, for reasons that I will go into later. This paper was just thrust into my hand and being a polite sort of a guy I took it and went for the train home.

Normally I would have thrown it away in a bin, or given it to someone else, but I kept the paper. The train was a slightly delayed in setting off and I found myself looking at this paper. I had no real interest in it really but being bored I found myself glancing through it but as I was glancing through it I got to the job section, because it was a Thursday, there was a fairly big job edition in the paper on a Thursday, I skimmed through the job positions, just looking at the job adverts really because at that time I didn't really know what I wanted to do. I stumbled across an advert for a counselling course, I had already thought about the possibility of counselling as a career, and this counselling course was at Bretton, which is near Wakefield.

It was a starter course to counselling, a certificate in counselling, I thought that it sounded interesting and so I kept the advert. I didn't do anything with it at that particular moment, but I just kept it, stuffing it into my bag.

I had already realised that I didn't want to be within Sales and I thought this might be a way to go forward, but I didn't know anything about it.

So about 2/3 weeks later I found the advert again in my bag and I rang the telephone number on it speaking to somebody in the admissions at Bretton Hall to enquire about the course. They said they were very sorry, but the course was full. I thought well, ok that's fine but then they said they would keep my name on file just in case anyone dropped out or if any more places became available, or even for the next year's course. I said ok that was fine and thought no more about it going back to my sales job and thinking what am I going to do, all those kind of fleeting thoughts that I was having at that time.

Within about four or five days there was a telephone call and it was from someone from Bretton Hall admissions saying there was indeed one place that had become available, someone had dropped out, as I said previously with synchronicity, these things sometimes happen.

I thought well if the place had become available, I needed to get on it so I reserved a place for myself to start in the September term. As I said at that time I was still working in Sales for a company in Manchester, so I went to my Boss, the owner of the company and said that I would like to do this course.

This was a part time one day a week course. Telling him how I could do, what I would like to do, that was to drop from a 5 day week to a 4 day week, bearing in mind that most of us didn't work a full day on Friday afternoons because the firm closed down on a Friday afternoon.

I said I would still do the same targets, the same amount of business that I needed to do but I would do it in 4 days instead of 5 days and to drop my wages accordingly, if he would allow me to do the course.

He was dead set against it, there was no way he was going to go down that avenue, so I handed my notice in there and then.
You know when you have times in your life when you find yourself saying something out loud and a bit somewhere inside of your brain says is that me talking, it's like being a third person in a conversation, hearing it happening but not being able to control what you are saying, curiously observing the process.
He was as startled as was I, as you can probably imagine, but I found myself reaffirming it and that I was adamant I was going to do this course.

I found myself then putting myself out of a job and happy, it was as if a great weight had been lifted from my shoulders, knowing at the end of my notice that I would be without a car, and all the other perks that went with the job, saying to myself happily I was on a Counselling course. At that time in my life thankfully I had a really good support structure from the lady who is now my life partner, soul mate and Wife. We had talked previously about my dissatisfaction with my career, thankfully she was in agreement with me before I had handed my notice in, and when I arrived home I told her that I had given my notice in, again strangely in a happy voice, which for a Taurean was really weird, as we tend to like structure and security, and as she again was very supportive and said, yes, go for it. We can cope; we can do this and that it was not a problem. So I said, right, okay, and I went through with it not really worrying about how I might bring home enough salary to pay my share of the bills and to keep everything afloat.

It still strikes me as strange that I could feel so elated when in fact there was no certainty of a secure future.

Chapter 2
Finding myself and were I fitted

The course started in September and luckily, because by then I was unemployed, it was free; I didn't have to pay the fees they charged, which was another synchronicity moment. It just happened that everything started moving towards this course, not being a dream but was steadily becoming a reality. Have you ever had the experience that something is just meant to happen, nothing stands in the way all obstacles just melt away, like those dominoes that just keep falling forward all along their path.

I did in fact find ways of bring an income in although it wasn't secure but things just kept coming my way. Over the course of that time I sold Children's Christmas books in shopping centres, Videos to supermarkets and high street stores, became a school Night-watchman: lots of spare time to do assignments, Chauffeur, Monitored advertising in banks, explained to people how to use the post office system and lots, lots more until I became qualified and able to find be employment in Counselling.

Although I'd never attended anything academic since leaving school, apart from some courses I took throughout my life in relation to work.

I had never been near any kind of University or any kind of structure which gave validation of an academic process. So that was a massive nerve racking event, having to challenge another one of my life's scripts for me, again from my Dad. Because I was always told, from an early age, that I wasn't necessarily good enough academically, well really inferred as being. I was the only person in the family who didn't pass the 11+, a bench mark of competence at 11 years old before you progressed to upper school or Grammar school.

There are lots of things about that life script that challenges me even today. At the end of the day it took a lot of courage from me to challenge those scripts and at that time I didn't know if I could do that. I kept on with it and I kept challenging it, even though it was a very emotional and painful process in some places of that year.

Challenging the scripts gives awareness which leads you to opportunities for change. Always challenge scripts even if you're happy with them. If we know why we do what we do then we have a choice to change it If were not aware then we just subconsciously react and have no choice.

I kept on at it and found that by doing the course I found out a lot more about myself and about my unique way of looking at the world.

My perception was growing, processing it through those experiences from my childhood and now beginning to realise how I could change them, knowing you don't have to have those scripts there are choices you can make.

The course moved through the process of the year and I found more and more stimulation within it, more and more aspects of awareness. I could see why my married relationship had broken down so effectively and what I had done in order for that to materialise and also my own responsibility within it. I should say that all this awareness and those ha ha moments, when the light bulb clicked on about everything that I was going through I put into the course, the coursework, the tests, the writing, it was not only a learning process but also I found a cathartic one. They say that every Counselling course has people on it who want to be Counsellors and some people who just want to be counselled. I possibly fell into both camps.

I found out through doing that course, why I'd had not really connected with being at school and with academic reading in general prior to this course in any kind of academic way. I found I was dyslexic which a lot of people are. It's a spectrum, which I now realise; a lot of people are on that spectrum, some very mildly, some very heavily.

Thankfully I am mildly affected by it but enough to stop me interacting with the learning process.

There are spectrums in all sorts of cognitive advantages and disadvantages I have found that connecting with that knowledge makes me realise that all humans are somewhere on a spectrum of some individual behaviour aspects.
These are not always a negative aspect they can have very positive benefits. I personally would rather have a high functioning Asperger's person making life or death decisions as they would be more objective and be able to release themselves from emotionally charged based decisions.

Are you on the Dyslexic spectrum? What do you think are the benefits of being Dyslexic or being on any of the other cognitive behavioural spectrums for that matter?

So finding out that I just had to learn differently was a very uplifting and cathartic process for me, knowing I wasn't thick I just learnt differently. This released me from the guilt and pain of my childhood in not performing as I was expected to do. I found also that in all my years of working, with every job I'd ever done.

The reason why I'd learnt things the way I had, in not going to college or university or any of those kinds of academic things. I found I had learnt by just trying things out or copying others, moving down a path of people asking me to do new things and learning quickly on the job, was because I actually learnt by seeing things being done. Seeing how things presented themselves, how they fitted together, seeing how things worked out in life learning through that doing process and not by being an academic thinker. I wasn't wrong just different. My skill was in finding the easiest way to do things; stripping things back to basics and making them work better. Seeing the patterns and logically sequencing them to make a more effective process.

Don't label people with negative labels make them positive, after all everything has a positive option? All the great forward thinkers were usually different or reclusive people. We only learn when things go wrong; we never learn when they go right. So being wrong isn't a problem it's just a healthy learning process embrace it don't reject it.

In order to complete this basic counselling course, I used those skills in looking at what other people were doing when we were carrying out the practise work, role playing, and the things that you do on these courses.

In all the role play that we did, I learnt a lot from the people who were around me, how they reacted and also how they interacted.
It was as though I could feel things as well as hearing things, feeling the words and the emotions that went with them, understanding more of the process than just from their dialogue and body language.

This different way of learning I now know is called being Intuitive, learning from what you feel not what you cognitively know. This type of learning is part of my on-going process in the work I do and something which I now successfully teach other people to do. Enhancing that way of understanding the Human dynamics can be most beneficial it's as though I have much more input in order to base my responses on.

I found my way through that course, showing myself that indeed I could learn, I could be knowledgeable, I could understand. The only hard thing for me was to write that down in a way that made sense to other people. My way of viewing the world is, or writing about viewing the world, is different to other people's because of the dyslexia. My wife used to tell me that I make a sentence that actually carries on all the way through the page. It didn't have any full stops or commas. Paragraphs are something that I really didn't understand, my grammar was terrible. Apparently if I wrote in German it would be fine because of the way they structure there grammar.

So in order for the course work to be done, I had to ask for help which is never an easy thing for me to do with the script that I had been given in my younger life. But asking for help also taught me that I didn't need to have all the tools and be perfect. I just needed to include other people who were better at things than me, using their resources and then just doing it in a way that made sense. I stopped using the script of having the pressure to succeed to be perfect, hence all those hours away from the family, finding that perfection doesn't exist you just have to be good enough and that that is ok.

If you always jump in first to do things and not let others help you then you can never be given anything or treated, made to feel special or to be fully loved.

I was lucky in the course, in that it had a pass or a fail. It didn't have any scaling points to it, but as long as you had a structure within it, you passed, which I did. I passed with quite a decent mark actually which I was quite surprised at.

I ended up with all this academic and course experience, awareness and extended knowledge in some sense. More importantly I also had the relevant piece of paper to say I have achieved it.

Completing the course with all these new things, these new tools or possibly some tools that I had already had but I didn't realise it.

I thought to myself ok what do I do now? Where do I go from here? What has all this been for?

When we were completing the end of the certificate, and the Tutor was asking us if we were going to go on and do the further learning with them, they were talking about having an organisation or some external place to go to use these tools and gain client experience.
After all counselling is not just a learnt skill but you have to practice in order to grow and develop. It's like learning to drive and never buying a car, so not having the experience to go with the skill and knowledge.

The College was talking about lots of different organisations around the Wakefield area that would be good places to approach and the Tutor at that time said you need to do something that you are interested in.

There is no point connecting with any organisation or doing anything in life which you don't have an interest in, because it won't be something you will enjoy doing.
You will also not be able to carry out the work with the passion and interest so being less than you might be.

So I thought Ok, what do I want to do and then I thought about the relationship breakdown and my interest in why people do what they do, learning that I did know a lot about human dynamics and I thought then maybe I can work with people who are going through relationship difficulties. Trying I suppose in some way to help put things right in other peoples relationships which I had failed miserably to do in mine.

I contacted a Relationship Counselling organisation in Wakefield. I sent off an application form, was invited to an interview getting through that interview and went on to engage in a day's awareness and understanding about what it was like working for them.

I met different people from different parts of the country, all doing exactly the same thing, going through this counselling awareness process. I found that I fitted in, but that might seem a bit daft when you think I was 41 years old.

No sorry, I wasn't 41 years old, was I 41 or 44 years old, I don't know. Time flies when you are enjoying yourself.

I think in some sense it had been the first time that everything seemed to just be ok, everything seemed right just like a hand fitting in a glove, as the song says.
To me this being accepted as an equal and it being so easy to reside in the group etc. was the first time in my life when I didn't have to question anything. As I say nowadays "it's just like pooh bear"

Enjoy the calm it does not always come before a storm sometimes it's just the way it is and there is nothing to worry about you can just relax in and enjoy it.

Have you ever found yourself in that calm place did you still thrash around in it creating more disturbance or just float and enjoy it. Thrashing around in quicksand just pulls you down even further stop thrashing start enjoying.

Chapter 3
Something I am finally good at

I think in some senses, as I said previously, it had been the first time that everything seemed ok and to fit. Lots of jobs I've done, and I've done lots of jobs in the past in different ways. I did them, and I fitted in and was liked within the companies and the people I've worked with, but this seemed just amazingly so like me, not something I tried to be, which hadn't been something I'd experienced before. I realised that previously I had been a chameleon type of person, being who I needed to be not necessarily being really me.

Luckily I got through that day's interview and started the course. In those days, when I first started, it will be over 14 years now, there were weekends away and you had to do 4 weekends in a year, totalling 10 days of academic work and you had then to do the qualifying course over a 2 year period.

At the end of the course there was a piece of written work to do which eventually led to the certificate. As I was going through the course you would have to do experiential work by seeing clients within the centre you were attached to. I went and did the first two weekends and, that is how this new part of my journey started.

They initially filtered the clients so that you were given the work that you had been trained to do. They had an initial interview with the client that then becomes an understanding of the work to be done with the person and what problems they are having from the client's perspective. Why they are where they are and where are they trying to get to, their goals – so they filtered them I suppose a bit like a triage service in A&E.

Mostly that all goes really well. Every now and again, as with all things in life, things don't emerge in that initial session that will emerge in the counselling.

One of the first client's I encountered, who initially it seemed on the surface to be a very basic piece of work. It was all about communication difficulties which had been explored in the initial session. Working out what people were doing around them, how they interfaced with them and why they were doing what they did, those kinds of things, one that shouldn't be too taxing for a new Counsellor.

I was working with this person and we suddenly found ourselves talking about all sorts of deeper things that I had not been fully trained in, such as abusive actions and those difficult areas of life and relationships. I suddenly found myself thinking Oh dear and immediately after the session rang the Supervisor.

A Supervisor is a person who I suppose I see as being a Counsellor's Counsellor, they make sure you are working to your level of competency and ethically. They monitor the Counsellor's work and help them if anything becomes too difficult, or unpick things which confuse or hinder the work. Or they have to make any kind of decisions or judgements about the work that you are doing. All counsellors no matter how experienced they are having a Supervisor, as these conversations that you have on a regular basis, with them help the work to be objective and safe for all parties.

I rang my Supervisor at the time, a lovely lady. We discussed what I did and how I did it and where we went from here. Obviously the alternatives were for me to finish the counselling with the client or give it to someone else who was more experienced, with more hours under their belt or to keep going with it, because the client had built up a therapeutic rapport with me, they felt comfortable with me and because of that were talking at that deeper level, but it was agreed I would have constant supervision to see that it, the work and they the client were ok. We decided to carry on with the work and with her help it helped me to understand what's going on, working with the Supervisor on a fairly constant basis.

That was, as you can probably imagine, fairly challenging in one of the first times of working.

Although it was something that certainly was fearful but it did take me to a deeper level with the work I was doing. I didn't find I was out of my depth. I didn't find that that I wasn't able to work with it. I thought I and the Client were at an ok place and the work eventually helped them in their life.

You never know what you can do until you try; doing new things increases you confidence and grows your abilities.

Use the power wall tool in order to help increase your confidence

What have you done which you thought was impossible. How did you feel after you had completed it? Make a list of your achievements and look at them if you're feeling disheartened with your abilities.

Use the Using fear constructively tool to find your fears so you can challenge them and grow.

In this way of working, I found that the listening skills that I had had all my life really worked very effectively and I was able to keep on going.

The process of helping that client and others to understand and make different choices in their life to move forward achieving the goals they set.

In all those days of me moving forward, I got more and more experienced. I worked with deeper and deeper issues and more complex issues and found myself enjoying the work and helping people, in a way giving something back. I suppose in my life, since those early days of 2000 when I started the journey has all been about that. It's all about giving things back to empower people, helping them because I didn't help me before. It's me trying to help make it better, so that people don't make the mistakes that I made in my life.

Being within an organisation that focusses mostly on relationships, it's been a good journey of ever evolving experiential processes in order for me to develop that awareness for me and the Clients I work with. In the early days, as all people, you make errors; all those kinds of whoopsies and we all do that. I found that in order to grow and develop, you have to make mistakes a positive learning process for me and one which I give my clients helping them to move through things more easily.

You don't learn if you don't make mistakes. You learn by making mistakes. So I saw the mistakes not as a bad thing. I saw them as a positive influence to move forward.
It makes a lot of sense for me that everybody has to learn, and in order to learn, they have to get it wrong to know how to get it right.

I said that a long time ago now. It was quite a surprising thing for me to think of in those days. A surprising thing for other people to think of now as well, as it releases you from the anxiety of getting things wrong to a positive thought of it being part of a process.

I found that people were saying to me during that second academic course and through the previous first course, that I had the way of explaining things that made sense, a simpler way of seeing things. I had a way of demystifying things making things simpler, making things easier to understand for me and then also for the Client.
Concepts and theories I could put across in a simpler form and people, clients, were happy with that. They were more comfortable with it. So I started to find my style, if you like, one that helped other people understand things and be able to take things on board in a much easier way.

I think in all the years I've been doing this, that is one of the things that I have come to understand, that people take information in different ways, massively different sometimes and in order for somebody to be able to give people an understanding, possibilities or different perceptions, then you have to try and find the right way to communicate with that person.

My sales background was, I suppose, a way of doing that. Of finding out how to talk to people in a language, a way of talking, that they understood. All my years of doing that, being in a sales orientated position or in a people connecting background, had given me a really good way of, and knowledge of, being able to understand how people understand, learn, react, or interact. I allow my perception to interact with not only the spoken word but also the feelings that go with the words, an intuitive way to work with the things that go on in the room. If it feels like someone isn't getting it then I will instinctively change how I am putting the information across trying to find there frame of reference.

There is a feeling that goes with this, whether it feels ok or if it doesn't feel ok, I trust it. Those are the things I trust, certainly now in my life, I trust how I feel and respond to them.

This feeling gives me an understanding, which may sound strange, but it is a very intuitive way of working. That feels comfortable for me personally and is, or has been said by clients, also feels comfortable for them.
It helps them, I think, to engage with me being on the same level no one being in a more power position than the other, walking with the person in this process of finding themselves and of growing and becoming.

This book is about trying to give people an awareness of how human beings interact, react which will help them to have better inter-connections and therefore lives. All humans are insecure to a lesser or greater degree so when we talk we talk through an insecure lens and in doing so say things which don't exactly say what we mean but tests the water of insecurity, so to speak

The cycle of insecure talking how people don't say what they mean, but say something else in order to try and get the message across.

That will become clearer in the following chapter, when we talk about communication. I think for most people it's about trying to get a sense of why they are where they are, how they got there, where they would rather be, so they can make some informed choices about.

I know that sounds very simple, and I don't mean to say that the processes people go through are not painful, because they are, but actually there are some very simple, fundamental principles to understand how human beings interact and react and if you know those then you can get the best from a lot of situations and scenarios.

You can have the life you want instead of having the life that other people think you should have.

I think in my life I've always, up until this change in 1999, I always tried to make my life the one other people wanted and never really the one I wanted. This last fourteen years or so, since the age of 40, I have tried to change that to a win win process.
I think a lot of people get sucked into that, to provide for others without actually thinking about what it is they really want for themselves.

Win Win the process of having successful permanent change.

I still find that hard even today stating my needs. If someone says to me what do I want, I find it very hard sometimes to say, well I want this or I want that, those scripts go very deep into our behaviour patterns.

I find myself more often than not trying to appease the other person, and saying well, you know, what do you want and I will fit that in with what I want. That's not a good place. It makes you feel satisfied that you are supplying that other person's needs are, but it always puts the other person in a position of responsibility in the process that they have to say what they want before it can be thought of and instigated. So looking at it from that point of view, I learnt a lot about those types of human dynamics and to be able to put that into some kind of language structure and frame of reference that makes sense to the different people I work with.

I have to thank a lot of people in order for me to get to this position in my work and my life. I didn't just wake up one day and realise all these things.
I went through a lot of painful journeys, likes lot of other people, and have been in numerous awkward places sometimes in this process.

My view of my life now is that if I like who I am today, and I do, I get a lot of satisfaction from who I am today, then everybody who has ever interacted with me – good or bad, right or wrong, it doesn't matter – they've all made me into who I am today and I thank them for their input.

So whatever experiences they have presented me with or things they have done, those experiences have built this person that is speaking to you in this book today.

If I like who I am, then I have to say thank-you to all those people.

I don't mean just the people who are close to me, or have been close to me, I mean to all the people who have interacted with me both professionally and sociably, that they have given me different views of life, different ways of looking at things, they've given me lots of different experiences. All of those experiences has brought me to the place I am today, with all my awareness that I have now, on which I help other people to achieve their goals getting those people to the places that they want to be, the future they want to have.

So every single person who has ever interacted with Ian Wallace, I need to just say thank you, because without all those people I probably would not be here today or if I was then not so effective or together.

This book is not just to help people understand things. This book is my journey, my way of looking at the world, which I hope will make sense, but as all things, if it doesn't, and then it doesn't matter.

As with all books, as with all courses, training courses, every interaction, some things we take away from those interactions, those courses, those books, and some things we just forget. That will be the same with this book.

I am not a Guru. I'm not an expert, no one can be, as if you are an expert then by definition you cannot learn anything more and we can all learn more. I'm just a guy that's had a life and thankfully, hopefully, is learning to make the right choices instead of the wrong choices.

So, in the chapters that follow I am going to give you my view of human interactions or my help with your path in this world, which might make sense, or might just get you to understand things in a different way. But if it doesn't help, that's fine. But if it does, that's fine as well; everything is just how it should be.

ENJOY!

Chapter 4
Communication

The art of communication is something we all have to a greater or lesser degree; its funny how this great and natural ability breaks down when we try to communicate with the people close to us. I have lost count of the many times well educated, good communicators have worked with me during the years and whilst working with them have found that they have lost the art of communication with the people close to them and this can result in creating arguments. Arguments work in cycle's they have a starting positing in the verbal aspect of connection but they will start initially from a negative emotion that has not been successfully dealt with. If you try to find the starting point of an argument it will be like the chicken and egg, process you will never find it. Because they are fuelled by an interaction and reaction process, namely it takes more than one person's input to actually have an argument they go back and forward and can be extremely hard to deconstruct as to why they occur. It's more helpful to try not to deconstruct arguments but to accept that all parties have a part to play in them and to accept your own responsibility in this process.
That will help to dispel the process of interplay and separate the cycle as blame just intensifies it.

A typical cycle that I see is insecurity; the diagram the cycle of insecure talking will help you to see it.

Arguments

When people engage in or respond to arguments they feel they are communicating their needs, albeit loudly or aggressively, when in fact an argument is a verbal battle between the parties involved and communication is lost in the struggle to win or achieve a superior position over the other person, and in order for one person to 'win', the other must 'lose', or be 'put down' in some way.

The only way to resolve this stand-off position is to understand why the people involved feel insecure. Why do I say they are insecure you may be asking? Well if we use argumentative language to win something, rather than calm discussion, then we must feel insecure where we are, and we shout or use aggressive language in order to move our position to a more powerful position to feel better than the other person that we are engaging with.

I use a familiar tactic which most Counsellors would be aware of, the Time Out process, in order to help these people to engage in a constructive way and not a destructive way.

Time Out is just a phrase which we use to help people understand the process. It enables people to stop arguments, as long as it is honoured and respected, check out the tool to understand more.

Another aspect of arguments is that one person may chase to bring a conclusion to the argument whilst the other will try to withdraw to protect them self. Sometimes this kind of argument can lead to violence; the one who wants to escape cannot, and so will lash out in order to escape. Similarly in some respect to a cornered rat, it will try to jump over you to escape but if it cannot then it will attack you to protect itself.

Negative and attacking emotions don't help in connecting with another person and also the feelings that are exhibited tend to mushroom out to others, think of it as the pebble in the pond scenario.

Pebble in the pond process

When both the parties are in the position that they can respect and honour this cessation process then they are able to move forward from this stage.

Then they can start work on why they need to adopt these positions in the first place, this then involves them listening to each other instead of talking at each other, as only by listening can you fully understand why the other party needs to adopt this position in the first place.

Understanding why they do what they do can then create the correct conditions to help them to be more secure and move them on to using the communication structure that they have forgotten. This enables them to understand each other and build a common communication structure to help them to resolve the thing they were arguing about. This phase usually has to have an aspect of asking not telling.

Ask don't Tell then you will always be working with The Shared Reality not just your reality.

Having hard conversations

When you need to talk to someone about things which are difficult then there is a process that will help you to have those conversations and getting a better more connected result.

Usually having good quality conversations with those people are hard because of difficulties in understanding each other or that both people have achieved a polarised position e.g. both are totally at the opposite ends of the spectrum in their perspective. Breaking down this process that I use with people helps to understand the individual components and put structure into the conversation.

How to have hard conversations

Chapter 5
Working from historical scripts

Historical scripts as a concept is not new and I didn't dream it up. It isn't exclusively mine. It's a concept that other people have put across and this is my interpretation of it, it is something that I have lived through, experienced and worked with over a number of years.

I am not sure that I am fully there yet in understanding these scripts and it is as always work in progress. It does feel as though I am getting to understand it more and more, with the work that I do and the situations and scenarios that have surrounded me over my life

Over the years, through all the experiences I've had, through all the interactions that I've had in my life. I've picked up, as we all do drives and processes of historical data and that informs me and you of our current position, current thinking or current understanding, which I call scripts.

We all have those experiences that inform us of who we are, how the world works, how we interact with it, a whole range of things that we take as gospel.

These scripts are mostly unconscious; most of them are not known and picked up from our peers - whether that is peers within family, within life, within school or peers within relationships. Whoever we see as somebody we would like to emulate, or trust, or to help us in our process of growing and moving forward in life.

These scripts are not just given at our birth I believe they have been given and adapted and rewritten and reworked all the way through our lives from conception. Because when we look at any difference to our own scripts we can accommodate it or adapt it to do some re- balancing process with that difference assimilating it into our own life.

To give you an understanding of that, I came from a very insular family. I grew up in a world where in our house it was just the family and mainly no one else and although we had extended family living with us, my Gran lived with us and she had her own living room, our friends and other people generally weren't invited into the house.

As I was growing up through that family, I unknowingly had been given the script that our family are the closed unit and nobody external interacts with our families house and that's the way the world works our norm.

So I am went through my life believing that everybody was the same, every other family works that way because my family had shown that to me – my script – this is normal for me and how the world works.

Now when I got to five or six, one of my cousins had a wedding and in the invite to that wedding there were only a maximum of two children allowed from each family were able to attend, presumably because of the cost.

Because there were three children in our family and I was the youngest, I was not allowed to attend therefore I was looked after by another family who I was friends with and lived across the road, I was there for the day and into the evening.

Their family was very different to my family and their family script was that anybody was allowed in and if they were allowed in, then they could have food, drinks and they could have what you had.

During the course of this day, various friends of my friend appeared and knocked on the door, there were asked do you want a drink, do you want a biscuit. Other people would come from their extended family unit, cousins or other people would arrive, and they would all come in without knocking. Everyone would be chattering and would just help themselves to a drink.

So their family script was that everybody is included and the family is an open process whereby anybody and everybody could interact with that process. All are valued, allowed in and accepted.

In the course of me being with them for that day, my script from my family was challenged because I saw a different script, I saw that the world could be different and it could interact in a different way.

At that point, then, I had the choice to redefine my script. If this was normal for them and my script was also normal for me or I questioned maybe my script wasn't the normal, or their script wasn't normal.

I had to do some calculations and reflection of which scripts I preferred and which script would be the better one for me. Although I know now that that's what I was doing, I obviously didn't know at the time being so young, naturally I just saw this difference and reacted to it.

When my family came back and I went home, in the next few days and weeks, I was looking to see and to test whether or not my family script could be changed to something similar to the family script my friend had, in so far as new people would be allowed in, friends would be allowed to come over.

I found that this wasn't so and that wasn't the way my family could work, it was the way this other family worked.

I then had the option to keep on with my original family script, obviously, when I'm in their company, in their house, abiding by their rules. But then much later in life when I had my own house, my own family, then I changed that script to say that it was okay to allow people in. Maybe not to the same extent as my friend's family, or their house, but somewhere in-between or on the spectrum of deciding of whether it's okay to allow people in, or that it's okay not to allow people in.

At the time I had no realisation that I was doing that. However I now know, with the awareness I've got of how families work or of how family systems work, that those are the things that people have as part and parcel of their upbringing.

Neither one in this example is right nor wrong but instead both are right for the individual families. Yet until any of us see difference, until we are offered a different script that we can see or feel able to take on board, that is not threatening, then we don't realise that there is anything different and we just keep going through the process and using the script we've been given, or instead we take the one that we've tweaked, or changed in the continuing process of our evolving world.

We are doing that all the time, every single day we are coming up against situations, scenarios, where things won't fit in our life, with our historical scripts and we have to then see whether or not we want to accommodate that change or reflect on it and do a kind of mid-way process or maybe disown it completely and just go back to the old original script.

The problem with disowning them is that we have, in some sense to then say that our script, or the people who gave us our script, were not right. This is a hard one for people to take on board; it's a hard for people to work with that process, because in order to disown the script we've been given, we've also got to see the people that gave us the script as wrong and the new script as being right for us.

A lot of people cannot do that they will return to the old script because it is so hard to challenge the script you've been given it could mean that maybe you would be an outsider, or you could be isolated, maybe not able to interact fully again with the family or the people who gave you the script. Do you challenge the family in order to challenge the script; you might have to be separated from them in order for all to survive. So as I said most human beings don't do, that mostly we fall back, as people sometimes say, toe the line, and allow the original historical script to just carry on.

Eventually, as I did, when I got my own house, I could then allow people in and basically make a new script for my children. Hopefully, they could then as they grow older, modify my script to their own script that they feel more comfortable with.

We use scripts subconsciously a lot of the time, this reaction drives us in particular directions. It's a guessing game most of the time, in that you guess what is happening in the moment, based on reflective historical processes of what has happened in the past and use that to inform you of the present situation, consequence a communication nightmare. Is there any wonder that we seem to get things wrong a lot of the time.

They say that something like 80-90% of each of our day is a sub conscious process, just a reaction. Scary thought isn't it. Try to unpick how much you think about in just getting dressed in a morning. Do you look for the fastenings? Do you remember where things are or do you have to search for them? Mostly we don't think we just do.

Every human being on the planet reacts this way, this is part of our growing up, being self-aware. That's why you don't put your hand in the fire twice, because you know it hurts, but also experience tells you, over the years.

That if you work with heat on keeping your body warm, that's its okay to have the heat from the fire, but it's not okay to be too close and have the flame.

Through that process of understanding you come to realise historically that heat is okay, because you need that to keep warm, but you would never put your hand over a flame unless you want to get burnt.

See the drivers and historical Scripts tool

All our scripts are completely unique. There is nobody in the world that would have the same script as me or the same script as you. Those scripts are our individual understanding of the world.

To give an example of that, I find now that when I'm listening to comedy either on the Television, the internet or as part of an audience, my sense of humour has changed dramatically and I don't laugh at the same things I used to laugh at.

I used to laugh at lots of different things, but because of my training, because of my evolving professional experiences of being non-biased, non-judgemental, being inclusive and accommodating in each person's culture, that it is their normal and they have a right to have that position.

I find now that my sense of comedy, my sense of humour has changed enormously due to that training and experience.

So I have rearranged my script to accommodate my new beliefs, my new understanding, my new awareness and that has changed how I now interact with humour in the world.

The historical scripts are what drive us all, a lot of our drives are possibly so much a part of us that they seem to be in our DNA, in a sense, in that they have been formulated from day one of your conception – not necessarily day one of your birth – as we take in a lot of information in the womb.
This is not something I can give you as a guarantee, as babies cannot talk. But after working with a lot of parents over the years it would seem that being in the womb can be a defining awareness process in our evolution.

I have worked with couples who have young children, experiencing mood and behavioural changes, when we talk about the reasoning behind this there is usually some aspect of insecurity in the child's pre-birth life as they experience things of this world through the experiences of the Mother.

This insecurity gives us all a process of testing the boundaries around us, to see if they are secure. This testing seems to form the changes I have made reference to. If for example a couple are arguing then they will normally see a reaction from the children in the house even if the parents say they never argue in front of them.

Never assume they, the children, cannot hear you as we all pick up the emotional as well as the physical environment around us to see if things are ok. Children are like sponges they pick up everything.

So if you take the view that an un-born child is totally connected to a Mother in the womb, then as she reacts to an emotional as well as physical stimulation it seems only reasonable to assume that the baby is affected as well, and will react accordingly.
I can only view that being born must be the most insecure thing we can go through, in the womb we have walls boundaries outside the womb there are none. So being born must be a very terrifying experience and one which could affect all of us for all of our life.

We are always adding to our historical data in order to keep us safe or to prepare us for what may or may not happen.

So scripts are enormously important. They are what keeps us on our path, what keeps us safe and sometimes sane. Also as they are dependent on what we've experienced; they could give us a view of the world that is like a prison, having no choices, no options, keep secure, which would be a very limiting script.

That could be like saying to a person that's grown up in that limiting script, the world is a massively dangerous place and you shouldn't step out of the door or interact with another person outside of this unit. Some people I have worked with have those scripts.

They can limit them and isolate them, if we are under stress and we don't know what to do, the rabbit in the headlights kind of a process, we will resort to whatever script feels safer and most appropriate.

Which is why some people can go round the circle of an experience twice; they will do exactly the same thing and come out at exactly the same place.

Because they hadn't been able to change their script, their understanding of that script or even their interaction with the script itself.

They just relate back to old habits, and the saying that old habits die hard is true, it is very hard to change who you are, because in changing you have to disown that part of the script that makes you, you.

Now scripts can be really healthy as well, they are not just negative. Scripts, for my friend, who invited everybody into the house, this may have been too much me. As we talked in later life he said he always felt like he was pushed out. Feeling there were too many people around him and nobody was giving him the attention he desired. Maybe it wasn't balanced enough for him either.

Obviously the more people in his family system the less attention each member can achieve. So growing up with the process that said I have to fight to find my position put him in an insecure process which he reacted to as a person in later life.

In all that insecurity, that although seemed at the beginning to be very chaotic, when everybody was invited in, was a very open system, a very encompassing system, a very nurturing system, as I see it now, but that system also had its flaws and its problems, but in a different way to mine.

So, when he grew up with the insecurity of where is my space, where is my place, how can I get that interaction one on one, that would change his world and his understanding of what he would maybe pass on to his children as an understanding of the world and his script.

All our scripts, as I have said are different, and all unique, naturally. Even people from the same family, when they grow up, will not have the same script. When they are children, having to obviously rely on adults to show them the world and how the world works.
Then as they grow up and develop they'll see more differences, then their scripts will be changed naturally. They will initially rely on the original family scripts to understand the world they live in.

Nobody can understand somebody else's scripts, as I've said, but you can interact with them with a sense of understanding and awareness, that's because there is a difference, you can be empathic with them to that difference and understand why that difference is there. It's best to be accepting of their individual script, by being non-biased, non-judgemental, allowing people to formulate their own understanding, the possibility of having a different script and owning it.

I was working with somebody a while ago and their script being that they didn't deserve success.

They'd been shown an historical family script that was bound by the following: you keep your head down, be a good worker, don't look for promotion, don't look at moving things forward for yourself, don't raise your head above the parapet to see that your different, that you might be special or better at some things than others and that you had individual qualities.

It took me two to three sessions to get them to identify and understand the script they had, because they were not aware of the concept of scripts. They just knew that they weren't happy and were in a position in their life where they were scared of moving forward.
They were scared of changing their world, of advancing themselves, either from a job function, academically or in any way. They did not realise that for all of us the world has to change, naturally and normally and we have to be able to change with it or we may become isolated, alone or out of sync with the world.

So their world became isolated due to the fact they found it hard to change, they'd lost a relationship because of it and we had to do some work on their historical family scripts, to find out why they were reacting. We initially looked at where those scripts came from, and whether they wanted them in the future.

Then we looked at whether they fitted them anymore realising within two to three sessions that actually, no, they didn't fit that script anymore.

Because they were aware or their scripts and drivers they then had a choice, they could move and amend the script, altering it by doing some work on advancing themselves, by re-configuring their script. They could look at, tentatively at first, to choose to go to a further education establishment, attending a new course, having a hobby that they were interested in, expanding their horizons and moving outside of their previously restrictive script into a new space.

That then made them feel much freer within their world of understanding, what was now available to them. Instead of limiting themselves they were now able to understand that actually this was just something that naturally happened and even though they knew they were angry, being a feature of restriction, when they then started working with that anger and that anger didn't have to be something they kept within them. They could then see reasons why the people in their family had used those scripts or given them those scripts.

So the fact that they didn't have to have those scripts enabled them to move forward and to become, grow and develop.

Which is, obviously, what all of us want to do in some way, shape or form. So that limiting script of theirs was then was changed, with the new knowledge and difference of the awareness of the work they had undertaken, to a script that possibly they will never be a high flier, but certainly won't be limited by their original historical family script anymore.

As far as I am aware, they moved forward and changed their world. That was a freeing moment for them, thus enabling their script to be growing, instead of it being limiting script. They now have a different script and will work the world with that new script until; again, they see a new difference. Then maybe they'll adopt or modify to another new script or maybe stay with the same script that they are drawn into. That will be their choice a completely new vastly different possible world of scripts, as I've said scripts are not always bad. They give us a view of how the world works and how we work within it, it's always a good idea to remember that.

As long as scripts don't limit you, stop you being who you want to be, then scripts are fine. They are not wrong or right, they just are and we develop and grow our own scripts as we move through the world as we grow and develop ourselves, passing on down to our Children.

Sometimes scripts don't change until very late on life. If we want to change, then we can. But in my view we just have to understand why we do what we do and then by understanding that there is a possibility that we can do it different.

We can move forward and create our own individual new scripts, our new life, and the new connections of diverse scripts that we interact with. We hopefully then will become happier, more content, more connected and interactive with the world we live in. Instead of living our life with the handed down scripts and it being a limiting experience, and then living our own scripts will be a positive, growing experience, which allows us to live through this process of being a human being in this world, and makes our future very different to our past, usually in my opinion a much better option.

My own historical data over my former years, as I've said before, told me that I wasn't equipped to be an academic. I didn't have those skills of understanding the English grammar and having all those frustrating lessons in my youth at school. Having the script that I had been given drove me in a particular direction in life, but now, after I've come through this ever evolving process of self-awareness over the last 10-15 years, I've realised that I don't have to be driven or directed in that way. My historical script or drive does not have to be my life.

We don't have to have those drives. I can see them, understand and be aware of them, but I also can adopt a different script which will drive on a different process or in a different direction.

For me then, these my ongoing new life experiences, can remove or amend those drives, all those past scripts and historical data processes can be changed, with me focussing in on exactly what is being done in the moment and how I feel about that, being at one in the moment, understanding how I feel about that different process of working towards something new.

I suppose my world, is in a sense, that I am constantly becoming more and more aware of my drives, my triggers. A lot of those are sub-conscious. As I'm now becoming more and more aware of them, my sense of myself becomes more aware and becoming more me.

Not allowing myself to be subconsciously informed and driven by those drives. Not allowing myself to be interactive and thus restrictive with those historical scripts and drives.

Rejection and fear

Feelings of fear of failure or rejection often arise from childhood messages that have not been rationalized or left behind. If people have grown up with a constant perceived impression (from parents, teachers, brothers and sisters or others in power positions in their life) of their being subjected to a perception or real imminent rejection or failure, the receivers of these messages tend to grow into adulthood with a process of having to have very high standards of themselves and others who are in a relationships with them. They do everything they can to control their lives in such a way that they do not 'fail' in their eyes. "These tight reins", when applied to a relationship, can often create the opposite of the desired effect, wanting to be looked after but not allowing others to do so, or have a balanced view of life.

The most usual messages which create fear of failure or perceived rejection are 'you're not good enough' or 'you could have done better'.
Sometimes these messages, or 'family scripts' can be subconscious not verbalized or even meant to be spurring the person on to achieve more. The givers of these messages would be horrified to learn the effect that they had creating this rejection drive in us; other times these insidious messages are given as a direct put-down or stated opinion, to make the receiver feel badly about themselves.

This need to control via put-downs usually indicates a person with very low self- esteem and emotional insecurity, putting others down makes them feel better by having the power over another person's feelings. This cycle of low self-esteem and the need to put the other person down stimulates the growth of the failure/rejection fear cycle in the receiver, as they are never able to be 'good enough' for the criticizer, as that could only happen in any relationship once the criticizer had built sufficient self-esteem to treat and allow others to be as equals.

Having endured this throughout childhood or in the teenage years, bullying has this effect as well, the message receivers can also react to a perceived or possibly real rejection by adopting a stance of 'yeah, whatever, its ok' don't think or worry about me or my needs.
In effect denying or over-riding their emotions and feelings. In fact their feelings in reality are more likely to be 'ahhh that hurts', they may experience it as that sense of shrinking or curling up inside, or going into a foetal position, is normal in these circumstances.
Sometimes this even manifests itself as physical pains usually in their abdomen; but they can't say this because the other party might reject them even more so they just usually put up with it, increasing this cycle of rejection.

This tends to make them accept the process until they can no longer hold it in and they then erupt in an explosion of negative emotions.

Often this explosion happens over very small things, the final straw or the last drop of water in the bucket, and often the explosion is also directed at an inappropriate person or event and not even towards the initiators of the problem. This emotional explosion can even be internalized and can result in self-harming in some way. Self-harming does not have to be something that the person experiences physically it can be that they self-harm by denying themselves pleasure or achievement. If you are driving towards a position of attaining a goal and then at the last minute you put something in you path to stop yourself getting to that achievement that can be a form of self-harming. An example of this could be the person who is finally achieving the qualification they have strived to achieve and they don't allow enough time to do the work, squandering the time on something trivial then this can be a sign of self-harming. This intense fear of rejection drives them in relationships to accept things but not to challenge them and they enter life with an enthusiastic aspect that they always give but very seldom feel comfortable receiving, getting in first, denying the people around them from giving to them as they can do it better than them so then after a period of time the partner usually gives in and stops trying.

This insecurity of rejection can be an ok place as long as both parties dance around it, co-dependency, creating security for themselves and in both parties, sort of like a see saw effect balancing each other but never being able to be fully together and both ok.

Co-dependency and awareness

Carers in relationships with others who need to be cared for can see this sometimes if the Carer has a big insecure moment, becomes ill themselves or emotionally unable to cope and tends to have to rely on the other party to support them through it.
If the carer needs to be cared for then they may find they drop out of the co-dependency sync with each other and cannot give each other the emotional support that they need.
This can cause a lot of emotional fallouts and both people would need to re-balance the relationship allowing the insecure person to then accept help and the secure person to be the carer.

Chapter 6
Breaking chains that bind us to the past

When we are in a negative mind set then it's usually around the fact that other people have impacted on us in some way, we then react to move away either physically i.e. leave them or emotionally by creating arguments. The way we react is usually because of our upbringing, our life's experiences or family scripts - what we have been told. When we react it's usually due to a sub-conscious process and not an informed choice, hence we react in the moment rather than think and then react.

These past experiences, scripts in our life, keep on interacting and interfering in our life and so control us in our connections with others, and the choices we make, when we are aware that we do this we then need to create a different informed choice.

Informed Choice is a choice which you make with all information about what the choices are and the consequences which may occur from those choices. This is better than using reactionary choices which you will at some point later regret. The process of an informed choice might be to stay and sort it or a reactionary choice may be to run away from it.

So we are always in charge of our own process and the only way to do this from an informed process is to remove the reason for those reactions from our past, this is what I call "Breaking the Chains that Bind us to the Past". For example if we are angry at how another person is treating us, say they are using words or phrases that have been used in some way to hurt or control us in the past, we may not be consciously aware of this so we just react to the words or phrases being used. We don't know why we are reacting; we just know we are angry.

This situation is very hard to change, unless we know the initial process by which it arose, and then we have to go back to that original situation and remove or alter our perception of it, the trigger that is holding our reaction, by coming to terms with it, looking at it and why it hurts or controls us so much.

Then by working with the initial reason, to release us from its grip, alter its interaction with us through our conscious thought instead of our unconscious reaction. In order to do this we have to release the emotion that holds us there, this is not an easy process because we have to take our responsibility within that experience, usually people see themselves as victims, my old self included, when things happen to us we tend to blame others, this then binds us to the initial situation, our feelings of anger build up a reaction process.

Which re- ignites every time we see or feel a similar process in our lives these are the Chains that are holding us. So to effectively break those chains we have to initially see our responsibility in the situation, maybe we could have said something, walked away, created boundaries or some other way of taking control, not being the victim. This then changes our subconscious process, although it does not change the initial historical experience, and it changes how we react to the experience, word or phrase, building a different reaction process in the future.
The chains are always emotional links so by accepting our part in the process it changes the emotion from one of anger (victim) to one of acceptance (love) and then we can move on, taking control of our life and stop the reactive process.

As I said this is not an easy process, to accept and forgive, and I don't know what I would do if someone hurt me deeply again, but I would hope I could see my part in the process and not build up the chains again which I did in the past. All I can say is that if you can achieve this positive process then you truly are living in the moment and that is so freeing to be able to live your life and not be restricted by the experiences of the past.

Chapter 7
The dynamics of Humans

The dynamics of humans are many and very varied. In some senses, human beings are vastly complicated people and in some other sense they are very simple, which may sound like a contradiction in terms. Obviously it is a contradiction.

They are vastly complicated because, as we go through with the scripts that we have been given in our lives, we have an awareness of the world with all the experience we've had, all the things we've been told, how we've seen it, time and time again this gives us our life experience of how we interact with the world and how the world interacts with us. We build them over many, many years, many, many experiences, in many, many different ways.

So in that sense, human beings are very complicated.

Our reactions are numerous and vastly complicated our feelings on the other hand are very simple.

The reason why we are vastly complicated is that in all those experiences that we've had and we are told about, lead us to build up barriers, build up a fear of things that we either don't know or things that we have experienced and that they have gone wrong. Human beings basically look at the negative side of things more easily and more often than they look at the positive. That's a generalisation – but in my experience and the work I do that's the way we usually work.

We usually look at things in a fearful way, or a scary or insecure ways first. We do that because, in order to keep us safe, our imaginations, our minds have a perception of what might be, always going to the worst case scenario first.

We go into the places where, if we look at the worst thing that can happen, then anything better than that or less than that is a bonus, which means we can survive, we can cope with it. We all do that very much from a sub-conscious reactionary basis.

The complication with human beings is that we all, in a sense, have different faces to different people in different scenarios. We call, or I call this showing 'masks'. We all wear many different masks.

The way I get people to understand this is that if we have a very intimate relationship with somebody.

It will never be as intimate as the relationship we have with ourselves because we know exactly who we are. We know how we feel, how we think, how we act, what we do, why we do what we do - sometimes we know that and sometimes we definitely don't - but we tend to have a much more in-depth understanding of ourselves than anybody else has about us on the planet.

Anyone we've ever connected with will never know us as well as we know ourselves. That's just the way it is.

So as we interact with intimate partners, people we have close relationships with, then we can never ever give them the full extent of ourselves as some of those aspects even we do not know about us. We will give them a part of us, a percentage of us.

That means that that interaction that we are showing them, has, what I class as a mask. It's showing them ourselves, but only to a certain level or to a certain level of mask.

Then we would have different masks, to friends, to families, to work colleagues, to customers or clients you deal with through our work.

Use the Mask diagram to see who you show your masks to others and how much of you they see.

All those different masks are okay and it is not wrong to have these masks, it's just a way of us keeping us safe, making sure we are not out of control or showing more than we would like to others before we trust them more.

So, as we build those layers of different masks, those different masks to different people in different ways, then all of those other people see a different part of us. They see what we feel comfortable with what are going to show them, how we want to be perceived by them.

If, for example, we were working on a shop floor of a departmental store and a customer came to us to ask us something, we would probably have the mask on partially constructed by the store identity.

The store gives us this mask, they might say this is how you talk to this customer who might be different to how you would normally engage with another person, and you might also wear a uniform which changes again how you would be seen outside of work.

This is what you do in this situation; you would never ever engage in that work position and possibly give the customer more information of who you are.

You may have a name badge that says your first name, but that wouldn't have an understanding of who you really are, where you live, how your life's progressed, all those individual things about the real you and it wouldn't be right for that person to have that because that is not what they are there for, they are just there to buy something. So then you have the 'customer' mask, customer service mask, or personnel mask, whatever you would want to call that.

However, with your work colleagues, you would have a different mask. They may know you a bit more, they may know things about you that you have chosen to tell them, or maybe other colleagues have told them. So they would have a more in-depth understanding of you, more of the real you mask.

Some of those work colleagues could be closer than some others would be, so those closer work colleagues would see a different mask. One might be a friend instead of just a work colleague, so they would be closer to you and therefore would see a different mask. They may, sometimes know you quite deeply, as you may have shared an emotional experience.

We do tend to give more of ourselves to people we would call friends, and sometimes that can be a positive thing or indeed a negative thing. As the more people know about us the more vulnerable we could be, they could hurt or reject us with that knowledge.

Then there would be different masks shown to members of your family, and some of those members of your family would even see different masks, depending on how well they know you, or not know you, or what you choose to show that person.

You may also, as I have said previously, have intimate relationships who would know you more fully in possibly different ways to other people, more sexual awareness of you and your life which would not be shared with others.

So, we build up these layers, we build up these masks we show, to keep us safe and to make us feel okay and secure.

That's where the world gets complicated for humans because we know us, we don't know anyone else as well, so what we do is we try and assume what that person feels, thinks, does. We do that fairly quickly usually. It's said that within five or six seconds we've made up our mind about somebody, we have made a judgement about them.

We do that because we need to keep safe, therefore, we initially presume what that person would be instead of knowing what that person would be and we do that all the time on a sub-conscious basis. That's normal, that's natural, and that's the way human beings interact with the world.

In order to connect as a human being with another human being, we would make up the story of what we don't know, to make the whole picture, a bit like a jigsaw.

So we have the real pieces that people give us about themselves and the pieces that we presume or we think we know and we make the picture up accordingly.

We will always get it wrong because the picture will never be the real person, how could it be. If you were given half a picture of a jigsaw and you had to make up the other half, out of four or five different boxes of jigsaws, all fitting the same way, then the picture would be a kaleidoscope of that person it would be a whole picture but not the right picture. The likely hood of who we call Jesus being white as portrayed in most of the pictures of him is absurd given the temperature and places he was supposed to have lived in.

They make his complexion white to fit in with the people who were looking at or trying to identify with him. The artists built the picture on what they were familiar with and not the factual aspect of him as no picture or true likeness can be seen, its' our perception.

In order to get the real picture you can't do that, it's impossible, yet in our world we try to do that all the time. So we guess, our best guesses, we assume. We make that up from our own experiences, our own understanding of how we've seen the world, or think that the world works. We will always get it wrong, it will never be correct but it is a 'make do' kind of reality.

As we interact with those other human beings, we cannot openly and honestly and fully interact with them, because just as we are showing ourselves as a mask, they are themselves as masks too, we are all wearing different and incomplete masks.

The masks will let us in to whatever level that person feels comfortable with and how much information that person feels comfortable giving us. As we move forward with our conversations with these peoples, in our interactions with these peoples, they may let us further in, or they may not, as we may let them further in to our world or not.

As we are going through this guarded safety process, to see if it's okay to let people further in or not, that's when it becomes complicated, the human dynamic. As we are guessing and getting it wrong, they are also guessing and getting it wrong. Then we are basing all our unique understanding, our knowledge, all our worth, on something that might be true or possibly isn't.

Perception and reality, and why it goes wrong.

We all do this, everyone on the planet, in some way, shape or form. There are very few people who would be completely open and honest with everybody that they come into contact with.

In fact, there was a film not so long ago about a marketing person who could not tell a lie.
He had to tell the truth.
The film was very funny, but in some senses, that's the kind of situation that would be really awkward for most human beings to live in, if everybody told the full truth, lowered all these masks and made the people aware of themselves, totally and fully it would be a very different and possibly frightening scary world.

From that point of view we are always trying to interact and connect with half stories, sometimes what I might refer to as fairy stories. If a person is a controlling person, they would never even give anything of themselves to us because that would be too unsafe. They guard their past and the relationship history they have had, you would find out very little from them and as a deflection technique they may ask more questions of you than you can of them.

When I am working with clients who are trying to understand the interactions of another human being, either in the room with them as a couple or a family, or outside the room, then in order to get the Client A to understand B, they have to understand some of these aspects.

That whatever information or connection or reaction they are getting from B, it will always be a guarded process. It will never, ever be them.

Human beings when they are communicating with another human being, if they feel as though they don't have the full picture, or if they feel as though they can't let that mask down to come closer, then they will react by checking that person out from a communication point of view and a perception point of view making up what they believe of that person or their interaction, that is where things will start to go wrong.

If B is trying to understand A but cannot understand them, for whatever reason, then B will do what they believe it is right to do. That will always come from an insecure not knowing position because they don't and cannot know everything. They will push at A's boundaries, they will check out what it is, sometimes in very extreme ways, and sometimes not in respectful ways. They may do that physically instead of verbally and that is obviously not going to help with the interaction and it will not achieve what either one of them wants to achieve. Plus B is being abusive and is not be in any sort of respectful relationship.

By B pushing at A's boundaries A will see that as B attacking them, having a go, not being respectful in that process.
A will then push back at B and B then will then become more insecure because they know less than they thought they did and so this cycle of interaction will progress.
They will make more of the story up in their heads, adding more perception pieces to the jigsaw, and all of a sudden, both people, A and B are completely out of any positive communication structure that is based in a reality, they are then in La La land, fairy story land because nothing is made from a full reality basis, mostly everything is being made up from a perception perspective.

All that will do within those two people is that it will just make their gap of understanding wider and wider. They won't be able to connect or they won't be able to connect with as much of a positive aspect. The connection will become less and less and the gap will become wider and wider.

Usually at the stage when I would get involved, it's when they have tried to sort it out for themselves and they haven't been able to do that they can't do anything to find a way through this confusing maze of their issues but they still want to be connected, so they will make an appointment to visit someone like me to try and get an awareness of their process, to be able to connect in a positive respectful way and try to understand a way to make that happen.

One thing that most people will say in this process that they don't feel heard by the other person, if you find this resonates with you then you need to sort this out, as this not being heard is a major sign of the relationship going wrong and the gap of non-connection widening.

As they, the Client's move forward, my job would be to break down those barriers, reduce those safeguarding masks, and try to get them to be more honest and vulnerable in order to be more connected.

To work on their communication skills to achieve that end, in order that they can then hear each other.

One of the questions I ask people when I work with them is 'Do they feel heard?', and most people who come to me don't really feel heard. That's usually really surprising for the other person in the room or people in the room if I'm not working with a couple but with a family unit, because the other people think that they are usually listening really well.
They usually think they are hearing but they aren't really hearing, because the person they are trying to connect with, communicate with, usually feels insecure to be unable to tell them the truth.

Sometimes the way I work with, what we in the counselling profession call immediacy, which simply means being in the moment in whatever is going on and reacting to it, I will say to the people 'Do you realise that this person, in this room, is feeling that they are not being heard?' and I will give them some understanding of that process, depending on what has just occurred in the interaction in the room.

The person that hasn't been heard, will usually look up, or look at me, and in their eyes you can see the understanding that somebody else realises, somebody knows how they are feeling. At that point, usually, the work will go to a very different level; it will become more connected, more honest.

The other person who has been talking but doesn't feel heard they will usually have a moment of release, of physical relief which can sometimes be either externalised as crying or an exhalation of breath. This is because by using this immediacy process that I use all attention has been drawn to the real issue between them and they have been really heard – possibly sometimes for the first time in their lives.

Now that doesn't mean to say that they would need me to do that all the time, it just means that I have recognised it, I have made each partner aware that whatever they are saying is not being connected with or being received properly and that we can change that process talk more openly, more honestly and at much deeper depths, which then starts to solve the problems of why they came to me in the first place.

It always fascinates me how complicated human beings make their lives. When in fact, now that I've had the learning I have had and come through this process, I think really life is pretty simple.

For me, life is just about trying to help people as much as possibly I can. Being content with who I am, warts and all, positives and negatives, and feeling as though I'm valued, respected and loved.

If I feel all of those three things, valued, respected and loved, then the world works.

In order for that to happen, I have to, in my interactions with other people, value them, respect them and love them too. There's no way anybody would give me those things unless I show them as well. It's a two-way street.
Take your responsibility in order to move forward.
I have to value, respect and love – also in an energy sense, not only in a physical sense –those people that come to me and connect with me. If those people feel that I am doing that, they are more likely to do that back to me.
Then we build a massively different relationship, on different levels, at different depths, with more honesty, more reality, less perception and presumption more reality, then people start to have a different life, start to build the reconnection they strive for.

Most of that process, in my world as a counsellor is done very quickly, the therapeutic bond as we call it and it allows people to move on enormously.

I say to people that I will never change them, and I never do. In all the people I've ever met in my work, in all the work I've ever done, either paid work or non- paid work throughout my new life, I have never changed anybody. I tweak how they work or interconnect with other people and show them that if they were to do it a different way, they would get a different result.

That difference, that they do, not me, just makes them aware of it produces a different outcome and then they can have different relationships, based on different needs and different values.

I am constantly fascinated by human beings, which is why I do the work I do. Every time I connect with another human being, they make me more aware; giving me more understanding of how complex, how complicated we Humans can make it.

I try, if they allow me to, to move them back down that path of awareness and understanding, to get to the more simplified relationships, the ones that work, with validation, respect and love. Then we can really connect as human beings in a much more positive way, a much more connected way.

The diversity of human beings is what brings us together.   It would be a very bland; a very boring world if everybody was the same. Thankfully, we aren't. We are all different.

In order to get on with another human being, we have to have those three things between us – they make the world go round. More often than not, when I'm working with people who are in the room with me, those are the three things, or one of the three things, that will be missing from that person's point of view from their relationship.

Not necessarily from the point of view of the person they are interconnecting with. B would always believe they were respecting, validating and loving A, but A doesn't see it that way.

Whether B chooses to change or not to change, that's up to B. They won't change unless they are aware of why they do what they do, and how to do it differently. Even if somebody's perception is different to yours, you still have to respect it - even if you agree to disagree.

In order to have that quality interaction with another human being, even if you don't understand them, you still have to respect, have to validate and have to love that person. If you can do that you will have good quality relationships with the people around you.

You can then start enjoying life more, be more connected, less scared, less insecure and then you would give more, because you get more. When you get more, you give more. Sounds so simple, doesn't it, but it really is.

Chapter 8
Systems and Surviving Them

As I was referring to in the last chapter, we all work at different depths, showing different masks, to different people.

When we have a collective group of people, a collective group is two or more, in a theory sense we call that a system. It's held together by a joined understanding, joined identity, joined belief or indeed whatever process that brings those people together.

That system has an identity, which each of the parts of the system, each of the people in the system, would radiate towards or be bonded by.

You might have a system of people who work for a department store, for example. All of those people would adhere to that store policy and they would also have a joined identity of whatever that store or group name was. Within that store, there will be different systems as well. They'll have their own individual system within the group system. There's the store, the identity of the company they work for, but then there will be layers of systems within that store. There may be shop floor staff, check-out staff, warehouse staff, supervisory staff, and there may be management staff.

There may be all of these kinds of individually different systems within that initial system.

As we work through our lives and through our worlds, we all do this. We radiate to the system that we that feel the most identity with or indeed feel most comfortable with.

As we are moving through these worlds within worlds of our life, then when we change or we do something differently, and we become different, we can then work within a different system structure. So you may have been a single person and then you get in a relationship with somebody and have a close relationship with them, so you go out together.

When you were single, you probably mixed with a lot of single people. Some of them may have had relationship partners as well, but mostly, more often than not, they would be single.

When you become a couple, then you will change, alter, and become part of a new system type which is usually more a couple based one. You will respond and work around the different systems with different couples. When that couple base changes to say being married, you will, generally speaking, work outside of that partner couple base and you would work more within a married couple base.

If you go on to have children you will then work around a system that has families. You may still interact with all those other systems as well.
You may still have single friends, you may have couples that you connect with who are not married, you may have people who have families and you may have all types of different systems within that system.

Use the system tool to see how your systems interconnect.

The problem that can happen with systems is that if you feel externalised from the system because of something that has happened which changed you or something that you have done, or maybe just because you are want to be different then the system can become unstable and awkward or disruptive.

We can see this with children at school. Children at school tend to be more comfortable in being very similar, very much the same. So a class would be a system. However, should somebody come into that system from outside, from another school or another area then the class system would have to re-organise itself to accept that other person.

Now if that other person was a person who was differently dressed different type of person, different belief system, from a different cultural system.

Something that sets them aside or apart from the class system then sometimes you will find that the class system will bully that person to either adopt the class system identity, whether it's the clothes or the group philosophy or how it works, whatever it is that bonds the group together.

If that person that is coming in cannot adopt that class system's identity, then they will be externalised even further because the one thing about systems is that it can't cope with different people or views within the system.
You have to either adopt the system rules or the identity or you will be separate. If they can be seen in some way similar with a similar connection then they are more able to be accepted.

That is why sometimes people get bullied. You might have people who are on free school meals. You might have people who are unable to afford the new blazer or the new jumper every term.

You may have people who want to be out of the system, who want to have their hair different or have piercings. They want to be different, be unique, to be an individual. This is not wrong, obviously, but the system, sometimes, cannot cope with it. The system would externalise that person because it could be a threat to the identity of that system.

As we are all working in these ways and we are seeing this kind of bonding process, in order to survive we tend to find the system that best fits us at that moment. If we are a person who has piercings, for example, we may adopt or connect with other persons who have piercings.

If we are a person who wants to wear a particular dress code, maybe 'Goths', punks, all of those types of people would have a shared sense of identity. It was where they wanted to be, where they felt they fitted that became their more connected system.

You would then work outside of that class system and try and look for people who you identified with or they identified with you, who were similar to you, same as you or had the same kind of ethos, look, whatever that was in order to make that system connected.

Now systems are at work everywhere and at every time in our life, this is just how human beings are. We like to interact with other human beings who are similar and we can feel very scared, very insecure, if somebody comes into our system that is not the same or would not want to be the same.

We would then have some reaction to that, usually not necessarily a good one.

We could push that person away, that group away, or find some of way of making them feel less than us, worse than us or at a disadvantage to us.

We might like to call them derogatory names, make stories up about them. We might even have a perception that they are one thing, when, in fact, they aren't, they are another. We would try as much as possible to push them away from our group, our system, in order to make us feel more safe and comfortable.

This creates a lot of the problems in the world today, to be fair, because most of the wars, most of the processes that people have disagreements over with other people is because, in my view, either they want what the other person has got i.e. land, minerals, wealth etc. That is because most human beings have been brought up to be greedy, they want something they haven't got.

We mourn the things we haven't got instead of enjoying the things we have got.

I don't think we do this in a way we would realise but the commercial aspect of life these days helps to foster this thought process. I was more concerned with the life I wanted and lost touch with the life I already had.

I excused this as wanting a better life for my family, which to some extent was true, but I never asked them what they wanted I just assumed this was so, not the reality just my perception.

Or that the other group cannot accept their belief system, their identity, cultural background or whatever the difference is. So we try and overtake them. We try to absorb them into our system. We try to make them like us, sometimes forcibly, if only we could accept them but that would go against the system base we have in our Human groupings.

This is unfortunately without an understanding that the difference of that person, that cultural belief or whatever it is of that system that is different, actually it would help us to grow as humans. It gives us more understanding and awareness and it gives us richness in a different way.

I remember, when I was young, I lived in a small market town in the east of the country. Up to the age of 18 I had never had any other food apart from English food; my Dad was a meat and two veg Man. Then in my market town, suddenly, a Chinese restaurant appeared. Not a take away but a sit down restaurant.

All of a sudden, there was a great awareness that there was a difference and slowly but surely, people were absorbed into that difference and had a good eating experience. They would relate this to their friends, colleagues and relatives that they had they been to this restaurant and it was really good food, really different but nice.

We then, in checking out another systems boundaries, went into that environment and checked out that system's beliefs, food, culture, giving us an understanding that there was something, as good as what we had, but is different and that difference was nice.

So we explored that difference, we can still be part of our system but initially this new system threatened us. Initially, in the local paper there was disagreement, there were people trying to close this place down. This sounds absolutely ridiculous nowadays, because most areas of the country now have Chinese, Indian and Bangladeshi restaurants, in fact a whole range of different food options exists today that was never around when I was younger, certainly in an oldie world market town.

Yet in those days, in a market town in the north east of England, it was a big threat to the local system.

Once we got used to it, after about 6 – 8 months, maybe a year, and then we started using it – or some did – we became part of a system that was within another system.

I must admit that experience grew my understanding of other foods and my understanding of different tastes and cultural differences in general which enhanced my experience of the world, outside of the restrictive world that I grew up in.

Therefore, difference is not a threat. Difference is something that we should attach to, connect with, absorb, but in a way that still gives that difference the respect and validation that it is okay.

How for you to survive systems - if the system doesn't want you, then you have to make a choice: eitherto be always in disagreement with the system, which is not usually constructive or to find the system that best fits you. The one that will accept you and the one you can grow and develop with.
I now love different foods and yes some for me are not palatable but the very experience of eating has helped to develop my understanding not of just food but of different cultures and worlds.

More often than not, we try and we keep hitting our heads against the system that won't accept us.

We then conform and we become less than ourselves, or get back into line, toe the line being an old expression that used to be said. We then can feel resentment, we feel as though we've not had our rights observed, needs met, our belief systems observed and respected, whatever it is that we have to have given up to remain within this system, and we still won't be happy. We will always resent having to be less than ourselves.

The wider system then won't grow; the system won't develop because we will not interconnect with the other system in an honest and open way. We will always keep a piece of ourselves back that might not be accepted.

So, in order to survive systems, if systems won't accept you no matter how hard you try and we do obviously, have to try, we have to find the system that does connect with us and does feel comfortable. Then we will grow and we will develop and will be happy. But while we are in conflict with our previous system, we won't do that because we will hold ourselves back, or be less than ourselves.

In that process we will always feel aggravated by the system and resentful of the system that we have stayed with and at some point in the future that will present itself as a problem

For such is the world that not everybody will accept everybody at this moment in time, so we have to do the best that we can. It is a shame. It is wrong in some senses, in my world, anyhow, but if you can't be who you are then really you can't be anybody but just a restricted produced and controlled person.

It is better to have the life you want, instead of the life you think you should have – or more importantly the life that other people think you should have.

You should be able to be an individual, to be yourself. Working within systems absolutely, but still retaining that individuality and though the system feels threatened by that individuality, then that is not your fault. That is the system's fault because it is not accepting, respecting or validating the person you are.

Never see that you are to blame because you don't fit. Find where you do fit or could fit, then maybe at some point in the future the systems will allow you to be the individual you are, be yourself and not feel threatened.

I suppose that's the wish list, but if we could do that, if all humanity could accept everybody being who they are.

No matter what their colour, their creed, their belief system or cultural background, then in my view, the world would be a better place. It would work together instead of working against.

There would be no power and control, nobody being the boss. Nobody being number one who is telling the system what it should or should not be and because everybody would be included in the system, there would be no boundaries, no barriers just the complete acceptance that being the individual helps all of us to grow and become a much better and more advanced aspect of ourselves.

It would be one human race. John Lennon didn't have it wrong with his song Imagine.

Chapter 9
A Better Understanding of Interactions with Others

If we understand systems and how systems work, or not as the case may be, then we can understand how to interact with people within systems or systems themselves. We can then have a better understanding of how those things come together, what their thought processes are, what their values are.

The more awareness we have of that system, then the more we are able to see it from their position, their perspective and also the rules and the norms of the particular system workings. We can then see whether we want to make a bridge from one system to the other system and then we can connect with both systems but neither one will feel threatened by us. We have to understand how the systems connect and interact because if we understand them, then we can work with them much better.

It's a bit like playing a game of football for example. You've gone to a football pitch, but never been on a football pitch before in your life. Never seen the game, understood the game, hadn't had the rules of the game explained to you.

All these other 21 people are on the football pith are playing football and you are then put into that game.

What do you do? Look around you and see what everybody else is doing? Well, they seem to be passing a ball. Okay, I'll pass the ball, but instead of passing the ball to somebody on your side, you pass the ball to somebody on the other side.
Everybody complains at you. They say 'What did you do that for? They've now scored a goal against us!'

You say, 'Well, what's a goal I thought you were just passing a ball'. They would then give you an understanding of the rules, of how they played the game and as soon as you become aware of the rules then you could play the game.

You would still fall down, at some point, on the rules of the game because there might be finite rules to the game.
You find then that there is someone with a whistle who knows all the rules and informs you when you are not playing the game properly.

Now, most times, that's okay because that person is there to not be connected to either side, they are impartial. They will make that game work to the best it can.

However that person may have a different understanding of that rule, may have a perception of that it. Maybe they don't understand it as well as you, so that might bring conflict into that game of football.

If before that person made a decision, he came to all those other people on that pitch, all those other 22 and said 'Well, I think this, what do you think?' And then they all came to a complete agreement, then the rules would be an agreed rule by all parties.

That person who had the whistle would make the full encapsulating agreement and there would be no conflict each person would feel as though they had been heard respected and validated.

But there is usually conflict because we don't have that awareness, we don't ask others; usually we haven't a full understanding of what is going on. We only have a partial understanding and that is usually the part that gives us more problems.

So, when you are interacting with other people, other systems, and other groups or even with other individuals, the main thing that you need to do is, first of all, have a common language and understanding.

Now that might sound absolutely ridiculous. If two people are speaking English, Chinese, Indian, French or whatever other language base you are using, you might say of course they both understand each other. Or do they?

In my country, England, somebody who lives in the south of the country would not necessarily understand somebody who lives in the north of the country. They may both be speaking English, but they may, more than not, have a different dialect, they could have a different speed of speech or they may have a different pronunciation, there may have all sorts of differences.

So, even though we are all speaking English, we are not all speaking exactly the same English.
I would imagine that this is the same for most of the world, within any country. It follows that, even if you are speaking the same language, you may still not understand each other.

Communication is so important in understanding interactions with others. You not only have to understand the language they are speaking, talking the same language, obviously, but you have to also understand how they interpret the language, how they see that difference. That has to be something that initially you have to communicate on a very regular basis, in order for misunderstandings not to occur.

You may have to sometimes repeat things, do an evaluation of what you have heard, reflect on what you have heard, to see if that other person actually is saying that or if that is what they meant to say.

Now that brings the speed of the dialogue down massively, because you have to check everything out. A lot of people when I'm working with conflict, will say to me, 'It's really kind of dragging this' and I'll say, 'yes, but that's not necessarily a bad thing because before you were misunderstanding each other. Yes, the language construction has slowed down from the interaction enormously but now at least you understand each other. The old saying put your head into gear before opening your mouth does apply.

You may say less, but you will understand more.

When they get that awareness and when they understand that, we can start making a difference to their verbal interactions. It is like anything, once you learn how to communicate effectively by listening, sometimes, and not talking, then you can solve things a lot easier.

Talking time

When we are trying to connect with other people, trying to understand them, even if they are from the same country or are in the same county in fact, sometimes, we still have to understand the differences of that person in order to fully connect in a more communicative way.

It is that awareness of that person or that system whichever you are communicating with, that is the fundamental aspect of communication. There is no point in saying anything to anybody if they either can't understand a word you are saying or they have a completely different perspective on what you are saying.

As we move forward through that awareness process of understanding each other, that's where the work can be slow but it also can be so instrumental on making those relationships work more effectively and positively. Instead of making your mind up about what's being said or understood, you ask them what is being said or your understanding, whether or not you've heard them correctly in what's been said or understood.

It then creates a bond; it creates a central process, which we are here trying to grapple with this thing together because just as you are trying to understand that person, that person is trying to understand you as well. It is a two-way street and you are both getting a good result out of it.

It is really hard to understand anybody unless you have that basic understanding about effective communication. Unless you know what is being said, and you understand what is being said, then speaking is ridiculous because it is just noise. It doesn't have any construction of understanding it's just noise.

Each person who is making that noise believes that they are right and the other person is wrong. They're not understanding me and that's not because I'm at fault by the way I'm delivering it, or the information I'm giving them or whatever, they are at fault with because they don't understand me. They should. Well actually, why should they?

How can anybody understand anybody else without having a conversation in a common connection, common awareness, common understanding?

Without that it doesn't work - literally. It is really hard work sometimes, to get people into that mental zone of trying to get them to change how they've done what they do because that is their normal.

To try and bring a collaborative effort, a joined- up effort, to get both people to understand each other and see that neither one of them is right or wrong.

It is just a misunderstanding taking away the personal from the interaction helps to deal with it.

By the time that happens, usually, people have gone down the path of anger and resentment and numerous different types of negative feelings. So then that just compounds, increases this process that we don't understand each other but we feel they should understand me because they are connecting with me.

Whether they should or they shouldn't, the reality is they can't. Whatever you deal with, with any conflict or any kind of misunderstanding, should have, could have, might have, are all possibilities but 'what is' is what you can work with.

The 'should haves', the 'could haves', the 'might be' the 'would haves', are all wish lists, they are not reality. They are what you would like it to be, not what it is working with any other awareness will never help.

As you move forward, then reality is a much better process for becoming more and more aware. This is because if you work in reality, what is happening, there is no confusion, there is no misunderstanding.

There is dialogue and there are questions, there is some joined-up process of getting to a point where we understand each other more.

That helps both people, not one, but both because if somebody doesn't feel understood, they are likely to be unhappy.

If a person feels as though they aren't understood, then they are likely to feel externalised, insecure, and separate to. We all, wrongly, assume that whatever has been done to us is being done to us because somebody wants to hurt us, harm us, and upset us. It is not always the truth, sometimes people just don't understand.

So we have to take that awareness back to the process of slowing everything down, asking questions, not assuming and then by asking questions and getting honest feedback, you get the reality.

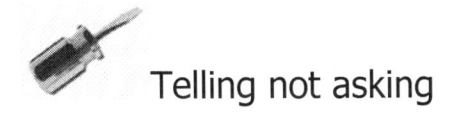

Telling not asking

I have had clients in the past who have talked an awful lot in a session, and I have said to them, 'but you are not telling me anything' and they'll say, 'pardon?' and I'll say, 'but you are not telling me anything. What you are doing is painting pictures and, unfortunately, it is not a picture that I understand'.

'You are using your colours, your perception, your imagination and you are painting it, but it is not really giving me any information of the subject matter it's just a lot of colour. Can we have some subject matter please?' and that really surprises them because they are saying an awful lot, but they are not really saying anything which helps me to understand them.

I have worked with people, who, because of their insecurity, how they feel about themselves or how they feel about their world; it is very hard for them to give their honest dialogue to me. They feel very awkward in saying who they are, what they are, where they are, whatever it is that they want to work on. So what they will do is use a communication tactic which completely does not inform me or explain to me the connection that they are trying to make, not giving any awareness whatsoever but they will give me a message or piece of communication e.g. I don't like being told what to do. They will say that up front in some way, shape or form, using some kind of experience or incident to say that.

They may then dilute it whilst still talking, painting more of the picture that they give to the person they are trying to connect to, which could be a very deep feeling or emotion that they do not feel heard or do not feel supported or whatever it is that they are putting across with that experiential process.

The person will again give me another piece of information on top of that, that dilutes it again and may say well it doesn't matter if you don't care. Then they will give another piece of information on top of that, another colour in painting the picture, 'well, I'm probably wrong in any case'.

They'll then give another one on top of that which may say, 'suppose I am wrong, really'. Then another one on top of that which might say something like 'Okay, I'm always wrong'.

What they have done, is, they've given the message 'I don't feel heard, I don't feel supported, I don't feel valued' and then they talk themselves out of that position and the person they are communicating to loses that real, honest dialogue within the picture that is being painted, which creates confusion and insecurity, just creating more of a problem within the relationship.

It's like reading a book and not having any character's names in it. You read the book and are then understanding the plot and getting used to everything that is going on in the book, but you don't know who the dialogue is assigned to. It is just a mass of jumbled incidents, stories, pieces of information but it doesn't give you anything about really understanding it.

So, as we go through these processes of trying to understand each other, as you can see, it can in a sense do your head in because there is no way you can comprehend anything without having that awareness, without having that common language, the common language that is really understood in so many different ways about what has been trying to be communicated.

Is it any surprise that relationships between human beings are so complicated because the interactions are so different and in trying to understand those interactions, those connections, even with people who speak the same language, is sometimes massively hard?

Now you can understand how much that would be enhanced, quadrupled, if you have two people coming together from completely different cultural backgrounds. Their life scripts, the way that they have understood their world, their belief systems maybe, are completely different. They may not even speak the same language, so those connections, those communication structures need to be made more aware and awareness brings with it clarity. People need to understand what it is being said and not feel threatened by it.

As soon as any of us feel threatened and because we are not consciously aware of why, we just don't understand, we are feeling threatened, that's what human beings do, and generally speaking initially we would react by either attacking or trashing the other person's opinion.

Once we understand and are aware of how things are, what that person is really saying, then we can do some work and have that connection, that understanding, that awareness because before that, it really doesn't compute, it really doesn't connect with us.

Trying to make those processes, those understandings happen between those two people's worlds, is only going to happen if people have patience, if people want to know, obviously, and if they are willing to take some responsibility for their own actions and interactions in order to make that person they are trying to connect with not feel as though they are the problem.

If we own our own understanding, our own awareness, our own responsibility in the process of interacting with another human being, then we are more likely to get a joined-up understanding of the whole picture.

If someone believes you are not listening or believes you are not interested, then they are not really going to give you anything about themselves.

If you take it on the chin, if you say 'I'm really sorry, I don't understand you and I need to understand you, I'd like to do that, I want to do that'. Then they are more inclined to say, 'okay, I'll give it a go, I'll keep trying, I'll slow the pace down, I'll try to become more aware, I'll give you more awareness of me, be more vulnerable' and help to make something happen, something to make that process work.

It is very simple most of the time to understand, as I've said, the dynamics of humans. We are very simple at our core; we just make it look very complicated due to insecurities and scripts. That is usually based on a need from a power and control base. That is usually because we want to be in charge or we want to be the holder of the information so that we can have the power and control over someone else.

A lot of that process is sub-conscious; it's not a conscious process. It is how we are as human beings but in keeping that information, in not giving that process or awareness to the other person, like in the football game.

The person who came on to the field might be really good for your team or even win the match, but if you don't tell them the rules, they are powerless to help and you're never going to find out.

That would be a shame because it could enhance your team, enhance your experience, enhance your world, but if you don't try and find out or allow them to try and interact and connect and understand, know the rules, you'll never find out.

> Well, in my world, that's a shame.

If we had better understanding of the interactions with others, I think we all could do with a little bit more of that, including me, sometimes. I am not perfect, nobody is. I get it wrong and I usually get it wrong with the closest relationships, as most people do, because they are very vulnerable, there is more for us to lose in our closest relationships, which leads to the possibility of more insecurity of rejection or loss.

Even people, who are great communicators in the outside world, don't communicate effectively in relationships.

People believe they should be able to, people who are good communicators, they believe they are doing so. Very rarely does it actually become reality, it's just their perception.

All I can really say is, if you want to know anything then ask, don't presume, react or push away. If you want to know then just ask.

Most people want to tell you they want you to know. Most people want to be part of the team, be included but it means that you have to ask. That is sometimes what human beings are not good at because it makes us feel vulnerable; it makes us feel as though we are not in control and that we are giving up our control.

This is furthest from the truth because in reality nobody is in control in any case, it's just a mirage. Nobody is in control – there is no control. You cannot control your world or anyone else's as we have no control in what others do or what life throws at us. We have to just act and react to what is occurring.

If you can try to ask others then you can know whether or not you want to be included, or a part of that awareness, understanding, system, game or whatever it is.

Then the world, your world, my world, everybody's world would be that much easier and that would help everybody on the planet.

Would it be a nice world if everybody accepted everybody else and they wanted to know about and value their differences?

They wanted to know and were interested about why they did what they did and how that worked and how you could interact with it and blend with it to grow with that awareness, just like me in the Chinese restaurant.

That would be a much better world, the one where we could actually say, 'We've arrived. We are as one. We are a community' and everything we have and do is for the greater good and then I would be out of a job!

That wouldn't necessarily be a bad thing. It would mean I had done my work and that I helped people to have a bit of understanding and awareness to the complexities of the human race, even a small way, which I do and I am happy to do.

I feel proud and privileged with all the clients I work with, with all the people I come into connection with.

That they allow me into their world even in a little way, if only some times in a very little way, but they still allow me in.

They allow me to understand them and that is a good place for both of us and then the world becomes, in that fraction of time, a bit easier for them and I and we both grow in the process.

Re-making Connections

When the relationships between partners starts to deteriorate it's usually a drip, drip effect, over a long period of time, sometimes years in which they don't even realise things are getting awkward until it is too late.

One partner maybe doesn't notice this drip, drip effect as easily, but the other partner starts to feel disillusioned and not having their needs met, when they try to express this they find their partner is so out of practice at construct communicating they fail to hear their distress.
This leads to arguments and the breakdown of the couple's relationship; sometimes the family relationship can still go on for a long time, reliant on one person resentfully "making the family work", this can be through the guilt of one partner, not wanting to rock the boat, so to speak, or from a feeling of responsibility or maybe a little of both.

They usually come to Counselling when they reach the end of the road and it's the last ditch attempt to make it work, not necessarily the best time to try to bring the relationship back from the brink.

No relationship is ever 100% happy but most survive because they have a joint purpose that they both want to make happen, so they put up with little niggles or frustrations which are quite normal in relationships. Also these days there is so much pressure on the relationship from outside influences, be it work commitments, society/media understanding of what they 'should' have, consumerism. This is especially difficult if their families are geographically or emotionally distant so there is little local support on hand to help them cope with these demands of the world,

Once the communication has disintegrated and they can only refer to the logistical aspects of the relationship, which one does the shopping, sorts the bills, looks after the kids, brings the finances in etc. Then the couple relationship really starts to be ineffective and detached. This can often lead to people having affairs

Trying to survive affairs

This loss of the connection sometimes does not even appear until the children are older and going their separate ways, leaving home, going to college/university etc.
When the couple have to relate to just themselves and how that interaction works, or doesn't, as the case may be.

This is where re-making connections comes in; trying to establish a joint stable connection without other people being involved it's what I call Quality Time

Quality Time

Relationships are always under pressure to find the time and energy to connect with each other; other things become, or are, always more important, finances, work, children, extended family commitments etc. This can be a deflection process also as doing things that give us feedback of how important and wanted we are which can be more rewarding than the poor Parent or Partner we have become.

It's more comfortable to be seen as good at something than not being able to solve something. If you are spending too much time away from your relationship check out why?

This being a good Parent is a message that we receive from most of society, family etc., and the interaction and responsibility of having and looking after children is very important and has to be done, but equally important is the link of the relationship between the two adults, if that diminishes then the whole family unit begins to break down. We are always bombarded with messages of not doing or being enough, via adverts, television, peer pressure etc. when in fact most people, even children, just want to be loved and accepted, not having the right label may be a drag but not having a mum or dad around will be missed much, much more.

"Quality Time" is a recognised and planned time which is not interfered with or lost; it is planned and does happen, unless something really important needs to take precedent, i.e. someone admitted into hospital or similar. The "Quality Time" is used to give the relationship time to bond and connect, the regularity is up to the individuals and as long as it is planned, and happens, then whatever time frame is good for them is ok, less than once a month might be too little.

Now we have to do something constructive with that time, and some people have no problems filling that time with something exciting and satisfying, but most people when they have lost this bond find it hard to think of something to fill it with. This is where, something I term "Surprise Jars" is helpful. "Surprise Jars" just means that each party has a container the "Surprise Jar" and they fill it with things, activities, they would like to do, not what they feel their partner would like to do, but what they would like to do. Then in the allocated "Quality Time" slot they take it in turns, and you can throw a dice to see which person goes first, they pick out of their partners jar, one of their activities and the person giving the surprise takes responsibility for that to happen, they organise it and makes the surprise happen.

This does two things

1, It shows the other partner that you care about them enough to actually give them a treat, which validates and respects them, and if it was something that you personally didn't much want to do then that's a double bonus, you're doing it just for them.

2, You can never be wrong, the activity that you are organising is the very thing they asked for, so it excludes the gamble out of making sure that the partner would like that activity, less room for error and less stress.

This Quality Time will re-connect and strengthen the bond of the relationship, give you fun, usually a much needed injection into the relationship, which we could all do with more of in a relationship.
Relax the couple and build communication between them.
This way of constructing a "Quality Time" process can also be used in numerous ways, with children for example, each child having their own "Surprise Jar" In Sexual Connections each partner having a "Surprise Jar" of things they would like to be done to them, which does not abuse anyone's boundaries, maybe a clothed jar and an unclothed jar, in bed or out of bed maybe, the possibilities are endless. Always making sure to respect and honour the other person's taboos, boundaries and values.
If we are constantly re-enforcing the bond and our connections with our partners within a relationship then that relationship will be much more able to stand the test of time and be more interactive, bonded and happier.

If there was a golden rule of what makes a relationship and having a happy and fulfilling relationship then the interaction of communication being effective, open and honest between the partners must be at the top.

Both partners should check out their relationship on a regular basis and see if they're needs are being met and that they are happy.

Control and Insecurity

Control isn't a problem in itself as we all have a tendency to control others; there is a very fine line between care and control. When care moves into control then that is usually paired with an inner insecurity in the person who needs to control. The controller will not normally see themselves as insecure they will usually demonstrate an outwardly persona of security, but internally they will be very insecure. They will usually demonstrate that they are in charge and the world has to work their way, this inflexibility will usually look to others around them as if the controller is doing it for the controlled person and indeed the controller will believe this, they may even not be aware they are a controller at all.

The way to understand if you are controlling is that the other person will not have a choice or their choice will be overturned by your view that you are right or your way is the best way. If you are showing you care and not that you want to control then you will flex to their request or see their request first as being one that you would want to try to meet.

Insecure, controlling people will sometimes create disorganisation when connecting with others who they are emotionally involved with, this disharmony will be very tiring to maintain and work with. They will usually find that they then complain that the person they are connecting with is very draining. By disorganising or giving different information to different people within the group the controller always has the upper hand, as no one part of the group has the full picture so no one can take control from the controller. Sometimes all parties have different understandings of what the truth is so the controller can keep everyone guessing and move or change the information to keep everyone separate and in ignorance. The information stream will always originate and pass through the controller; they will isolate and divide others to remain the one person everyone can connect to.

The people who are being controlled never usually know they are being controlled; it's a drip, drip, process over months or years resulting in being gradually drained of confidence and or self-esteem. They will usually find they are not able to make decisions or carry out functions that they used to have no problem in doing.
They will feel as though they have to ask the controller to check they are making the right choice or decision, this is sometimes the first understanding that you are with a controller.

Controllers will never be able to take responsibility for their actions and they will never see themselves as the problem. Controllers generally never fully interact with the person they are controlling they will never fully integrate with the relationship and they will always have a 'reserve' person in the running to be the next controlled person or will control as many people as possible and one will be the favourite until they lose the position and another takes over as the favoured person. If you have a relationship with a controller it is unlikely they will suddenly change voluntarily, as they are unaware that they cause the problem, they are merely 'helping', or 'doing it for you'. This may not be a conscious thought process but maybe it's a sub-conscious process they use to keep themselves safe. If they are conscious of what they are doing they will not change their behaviour when challenged by you when you say that they are hurting you.

They may say they will change and they may for a while but then they will return to the position as before. When one element of a system changes, everything else must do, just by the laws of science, so the secret is for both sides to become aware that change needs to be put in place.

The Elements of Control and Manipulation

People who have a tendency to control will display some or all of the aspects below; with observation and practise they become easier to recognise.

They will never take responsibility for their actions and it will always be someone else's fault, even with the smallest of things when it is plain that it was their fault. It could be a simple as them leaving the fridge door open or not remembering to put the light off.

They will always try to isolate you from other friends, family etc. Making you feel guilty that you are spending time with other people and not them. Possibly saying things like they were planning to take you out but then something always happens to make it impossible to actually go and then it's too late to re-arrange and go out with your friends.

They will never give without them getting something more back in return. An example might be that they take you out for a meal but then not contribute to the on-going household expenses if they live with you.

They will build you up and drop you down. They may say your wonderful to your face and then put you down in front of your mates or family.

They will make you believe that you are the controller not them or that you have the issues they have.

Finally they will make you believe that you cannot do without them and you will give up any rights you have in order to keep the relationship alive, making you dependant on them to live.

If your partner scores more than 3 of these then you're with a Controller, if they score under three you're with a possible future controller.

The Characteristics of a controller

Controllers will always be weak people, this may sound a silly or stupid statement, but controllers are weak, they need you to make them feel or seem to be strong. Controllers will always single out strong people, yes that's you, because the stronger the person they are trying to control the greater the controllers strength.

Controllers generally speaking will have little they connect with from their past, possibly loners when you meet them and then they become very sociable trying to muscle in on your friends and family making everyone feel they are great people, will do anything for anyone, apart from you.

This builds the picture of a nice, sociable person, so that when in the future you talk to others about them being wrong or a problem, they will not believe you and so making you feel you are the problem, you must be wrong. This is so they can isolate you even further and control you even more, making you think that you are mentally un-sound or incapable of seeing things in reality.

Of course control comes in many shapes and sizes, and whilst many controllers are simply repeating a family 'script' of taking charge of others; the level of control they exert varies from something you might call being nosey or in your face to a level of not being allowed to think for yourself and the many levels in between.
A few controllers are extreme to the point of posing a serious threat to those under their control, we'll call them super-controllers.
To the super-controller it's all a big game; they get pleasure out of hurting other people and the more the pain the more the pleasure. Super-controllers never have real feelings for anybody; you cannot have feelings for people if you get pleasure out of hurting people you are supposed to care about or making people believe they are bad or wrong.
Having feelings for people means you must care and super-controllers don't, it's just a game, a very horrible game but still just a game to them.

They never stop until the person they are trying to control is so dependent on them that they will do literally anything for them, they will take and take till there is no more then throw you away but never let you go always connecting to you with a thread, possibly through the children.

Super-controllers will never allow you to leave unless they are finished with you but even then they come back to just make your life hell again, just because they can. They will strip away any dignity you have, any sense of worth or value that you have in yourself, take away all that is dear to you and leave you a shadow of your former self. They will put you down; remove your confidence and self-esteem until you are unable to make the smallest of choices. They will take away any options you have to leave, controlling you financially and making you a prisoner in your own home or even worse making you believe outside your door is unsafe, making you a voluntary prisoner.
Thankfully, super-controllers are rarer than the other sorts.

Trying to change a Controller

The only way to change the process of a controller is to put firm boundaries in place, firm ones being ones that don't move even if they are trying to make you feel guilty.

Guilt is one of the major tools of a controller, guilt is a feeling which is used to try to prise, move or change the outcome. If someone is trying to make you feel guilty then it's almost always because they don't respect your views or position and want you to accept theirs.

Challenge their controlling behaviour and if they don't accept they are wrong then give them facts, not feelings, as to why they are wrong, controllers don't like black and white options as they cannot move them.

Take responsibility of your own life and decisions, remember they are not controlling you, you are letting them control you, this way of looking at things gives you the understanding that you are not a victim and that you do have a choice.

If they cannot or will not change then the only final leverage is that the relationship is over unless they give you respect for yourself and others, only use this one if you mean it, you cannot back down from this one if you do then they will just have succeeded in controlling you even more.

Control does not have a Gender it comes in both male and female options.

Chapter 10
Intuitive processes

For me when it first happened, this intuitive process, it was a very weird, a very confusing state to be in. It happened a while ago now. I was working with somebody who was going through a lot of loss. Not in the sense of just people passing over, although there had been, but also the loss of job, loss of a relationship. There were a number of different losses and grief processes going on at the same time for them.

Working with Loss

As I was working with that person, I worked with them naturally and normally as I would do with anyone. As I processed what had transpired with them after the session, my interactions and what I'd been doing, it felt very much like a third part of me was there, there was something separate to me. I was still holding a lot of feelings and emotions form the session.

When I started to reflect on them, I realised that something in my past, in my history, in my experiential learning, had connected with the subject that we were working with.

From my point of view, I reflected that if I was feeling something from my past, or had not processed something from my past properly then working with the client with a similar feeling or a similar type of feeling, then that in a sense could cloud the work. It left me with this resonating feeling of emotion of loss.

As I was working more with the counselling process I was doing more and more reflecting, as we do acquiring more and more awareness, I found that I could work on understanding of the Client more by actually relating to the fact that the client had had this effect on me.

It gave me like a barometer to say, okay this is a piece of work I need to do on me, because I was still holding it after the client had left with the work I had been doing with them, we call, in Counselling terminology, the process of transference.

That was a really helpfully intervention for me as I grew in my awareness and my experience of the work I do.
It meant that every time I had this resonating feeling, this piece that was still keeping hold of me, this hook into me, for want of a better word, it created awareness to work on that process, work on that piece of my life and my experience.

I am constantly working through that process of reflection as a Counsellor, and I do that because I don't think that personally, for me, you ever work through everything in your life your experiences. I think everything has an element of being 'kept', if you like, resonating less and less over time and disrupting less and less as you become more and more aware of it, but I don't think you ever lose it completely, I don't think that can happen.
So, in my counselling world I am aware of that and I work with it when it arises, but until it arises, the third aspect of me which is evaluating the dialogue between me and the other person, in a sense, doesn't interact in the room just reflects afterwards on what has happened.

This gives me a lot of very deep understanding of what is in the dialogue that I'm having with someone or the interaction we are going through. It connects with me at different levels in my psyche. Obviously we take the entire world in through our five senses. There is also an energy in my world, an energy transfer system, whereby if I'm working with somebody, I don't only take in the dialogue and the body language and all the other things that are going on around the interaction, I also have this separateness of me, that can take in the feelings and emotions that's also driving through the process of interaction with another person.

In that sense, I challenge my concept, my view of that dialogue with this other input, with this other sense and aspect of me.

If, for example somebody was giving me facial expressions and body language of having a happy smiley face and then their process of their words were about deep emotional situations that's happened to them, then on top of that, this third aspect of me would be connecting with the energies that's being transferred between the two of us and it might give me another feeling of anxiety or depression, low mood, or any of those types of feelings. I would use that to supplement the information that was coming through from my other five senses. That would enable me to ask questions whether or not that person was able to be honest or open or whether or not there was something else that I needed to be working with underneath the surface.

There are only so many feelings and emotions that a human being can have if you take it back to basics. If we have experienced something along the lines of those feelings and emotions then we can get an understanding of what somebody else is going through.

We will never know exactly what they are going through, because every situation is different, as I've said, but we can get an empathic response to that person and that connection. That helps in the course of my work, obviously, but also in the course of my life. Because I am more aware, the more I understand and the more I understand, the more I am aware. It's a kind of circular type of process.

In my world, my understanding, my reflection of that world, it helps me to understand, it helps me to cope and be alongside another person's world. Not judging, being biased, accepting of and connecting with those people that I interact with.

As we, the Client and I are moving forward with the work, I find that this being intuitive helps the bonding process to the Client and helps the therapeutic connection with the Client. It gives the Client an understanding that I can be aware of where they are, even if I don't understand exactly where they are. It also gives the focus of our work a much deeper and quicker connection.

I have people that say to me, 'I've told you so much more that I have ever told anyone else', also 'I don't understand why I feel so calm, why I feel so still, why I'm able to talk about these things with you' but never been able to do that with other therapists in the past.

I also get people who relate easily to this bonding process because it connects so quickly and so deeply, it scares them sometimes and they possibly find it hard to be around me, because they reduce their boundaries, they reduce their firewalls, whatever you want to call that – and that can be really scary. How did someone get underneath my radar so quick? Is possibly a thought they may have?

If people are very security based, i.e. they need to be emotionally safe; this can be a very awkward process for them to interact with. So I do realise that this has, as with all things, sometimes a negative response, but on the whole it has a positive aspect of an emotional connection which is beneficial for the client.

I suppose my world, when I'm interacting with other people, is one where to some extent I feel the things that they go through or have gone through, that for me also cannot be such an easy a place, to hold on to those feelings.

Imagine a world for example where you go to the theatre and there is a musical on. You have got the components of the musical, the orchestra playing the tunes, the people up on the stage singing and dancing and interacting with the story process and that can be quite an intense emotional experience.

Now imagine, on top of that, overlay on that, you felt the emotion that every singer was portraying, every person playing an instrument was experiencing, that experience can be so intensive but it can also be so rich and fulfilling. Imagine a world like that and it might give you an idea of the kind of depth and awareness and understanding that this intuitive process can materialise.

We take everything in by the five senses naturally, but there is also something else. Call it intuition, sixth sense, but it gives us more than the information that we've have gained through just the five senses. I can't bottle it and I can't tell you how it looks or how it feels in its entirety, only giving you a snapshot of how I perceive it. Other people presumably perceive it differently but in my world, in my understanding, it helps so much with the work I do and with the time I spend with people helping them in the process to understand their world.

But as I've said, it does have an element of reality for me in a sense that the feelings or the emotions that I'm interacting with, I do feel them, and that can be a very awkward place sometimes, taking on of other people's feelings and emotions. It can be sometimes hard to connect with that and still remain emotionally separate from it.

Over the years, as my work has progressed, it becomes easier to do, it never becomes easy, but it becomes easier. As long as I feel I am benefiting the person or persons I am working with, then for me that is a positive role and one that gives them help and is a beneficial experience.

In this separateness that I have which understands things from different perspectives I do feel that it is still a part of me and I do feel it has a part to play in this process.
In this interaction I have to be vulnerable because even though I am picking these things up from the person or persons I am working with, in a sense I give them my feelings as well.
Which I must say from a counsellor, or a therapist's point of view, can be fairly scary. In that connection they understand me, possibly as much as I understand them at that moment, which creates the therapeutic bond, but also makes me vulnerable to them, picking up on my interactions. Whether they understand that or can feel that or can make sense of it depends on the person.

If they can, then they can realise that I am as vulnerable as them. In that moment of joining together, that moment of connection, it can be a very safe place for all parties but it can also be a very scary place as well.

In order to have that connection you have to trust the other person, that they would not trash it, utilise it against you, because there is an outcome to be achieved, there is a need to help and that is, obviously one of the big drivers.

As I've said, I've gone through a lot of awareness over the years of doing this and I am still becoming more and more aware. I don't think you ever stop that.
I think the more I connect with it, being intuitive, the more I understand it, this process of working within my world and my life. It enhances my work and everything it becomes more real.

Another example of that might be, imagine walking in a wood, being just out in the country. You see the colours, the trees, you hear the sound, the smells and you might even taste the air around you. But imagine that you are doing all those things but you also see the individual colours of the leaves of the trees. Seeing the light greens and the dark greens and you can hone in on every individual colour and hold it, it becomes then more intense an experience. You become an integral part of that world. Instead of being involved in clarifying your thoughts and clearing your mind, in that one moment you are connected to anything and everything in that place, in that time. Think about how freeing and invigorating that is – but scary.

You are not separate to but are part of, melting into it, it becomes you and you become it a totally shared experience.

It's an interesting concept and one that I don't fully understand yet, but one that I am trying to adapt to and include in my world, and my work.

Not just because it gives me a sense of satisfaction and connectedness but it also helps in understanding other people's realities, other people's worlds. If that helps them to achieve their procession; that they are looking to engage with, looking to understand in the work we do then that for me is what it is all about.

As I have said I can't bottle it I can't tell you how it looks or feels in its entirety, I can only give you a snapshot of how I perceive it. Other people presumably perceive it differently but in my world, in my understanding, it helps so much with the work I do and with the time I spend with people helping them to understand their world.

That is my view of Intuitive Therapy and hopefully it makes sense when you read this. If it would be helpful for you to understand a different way of seeing things that could make you more connected too and a part of, more immersed in yours or other peoples worlds.

If you are interested in developing your own intuitive process then please feel free to drop me a line so I can advise you as to when the next course is being run. I would be more than happy to have a conversation about using this cutting edge process with possible advantages in any interaction that we have with humans in general not just within the Counselling fraternity.

For more information please contact the web site which is at.

www.intuitivetherapy.co.uk

Chapter 11
In the Now

The aspect of this 'In the Now' concept is not unique to me and not something I invented. But it is something about me utilising those aspects of informing me and helping to understand the dialogue and the process between me and the other party in a much more holistic way. This gives me more sense and awareness of that dynamic, the interaction between us which makes it more real, powerful and aware.

I suppose in my world I am constantly becoming more and more aware of not only my drives, triggers but also other peoples as well. A lot of those drives are a sub-conscious process as I have said. As I'm becoming more and more aware of them, my sense of self, my sense of the aspect of me, the third person, that needs to be separate to that interaction, becomes more aware also. As with all things the more I learn the more I know the more I know the more I learn, it's a continuous cycle.

So this third part of my awareness is not allowing itself to be driven by those historical drives, merely observing the process of the interaction. Not allowing myself to be restricted, or obstructed by those drives.

This third part just sees what is going on in the moment, in the now and seeing what is going on through the connection that I am making.

For me, initially, when it first happened, was a very weird moment indeed, a very confusing state to be in. It was as if all time had frozen and each second was more than a minute. I became aware that everything was clearer and things became focussed in a much more intense way. I could somehow look around and see things, which previously I would have probably missed, they became more defined. I found that my thoughts also were much clearer and I could evaluate things in a different way. I was not thinking of what had happened previously or what was to become I was just frozen in the moment.

This 'In the Now', is a calm peaceful place which encompasses a sense of being separate to but also being connected with. When I'm working within this process, I find that it also gives me a sense of satisfaction also in that calmness, not a smug I know satisfaction, but a deeper sense of being connected. I am not always 'In the Now' when I'm working with another person. I sometimes work with it on my own; some people might class this as being in meditation, the situation of sitting with yourself.

For me 'In the Now' is a process by which I can now include a third part of myself within the interaction or the dialogue that I am having.

That part is separate to this dialogue or the interaction I am having, but I am watching it and listening to it trying to understand it. I am also interacting with it to give a sense of the other person's viewed position. Not just by dialogue and body language, but also by the emotional content that's moving backwards and forwards through this interactive process.

So this 'separate to' position I adopt, is in a quiet space within the room. In a space where there is no previous interaction, or previous knowledge, or previous experiential process from my life or my drives. It is an observer position, whereby it is experiencing everything in the moment as Client relates to me and me to them.

It is not a place where I think I get to all the time, but it is a place I am getting to more and more. Over the years, through all the experiences I've had, through all the interactions I've had in my life that I've picked up, as we all do, drives and processes of historical data and that informs our current position, thinking or current understanding.

We then use that understanding subconsciously. A lot of the time this reaction drives us in particular directions. It is a best guess process trying to put the jigsaw of understanding together. You guess what is happening in the moment based on reflective processes of what has happened in the past.

Although I don't meditate in the strictest sense of the word, I do what I class as 'daydream'. I'll go off somewhere in my head, processing things and working with things, which I know is strictly not meditation because for me mediation is about being in the moment and not being aware of anything but a blank canvas. I suppose for me as I said it is a self-reflecting process of like being in a daydream.

Sometimes I do find myself meditating in a place where the daydream doesn't have to have anything, it can just be still, it can just be calm and it just gets lost in its own process.
That can be a really interesting time and also a rejuvenating time.
It restores my balance, restores my energy, my reality on the world as well. Sometimes this is when my most productive thoughts happen and issues and problems are worked out.

By that I mean that the more I am able to understand me as a human being, the more I am able to understand other people as well. Although we are all separate, we are all different; there are a lot of commonalities, lots of threads that are very similar within feelings and emotions.

There are only so many feelings and emotions that a human being can have if you take it back to basics.

If we have experienced something in our life along the lines of the feelings and emotions that a Client is processing in the room then we can get an understanding of, be empathic with, something that somebody else is going through.

We will never know exactly or completely what they are going through, because every situation is different, as I've said, but we can get an empathic response to that person and that connection. That helps in the course of my work, obviously, but also in the course of my life.

Because I am more aware, the more I understand and the more I understand, the more I am aware. It's a kind of circular type of process that I find very interesting in my world and also my life but also in being aware of other people's lives. So, being 'In the Now' is such a simple thing, but to get there can be a complicated process as with most things I suppose.

In my world, my understanding, my reflection of the world, it helps me to understand, cope and belong to or connected with another person's world. Not judging, not being biased, accepting of and connecting with, those people that I interact with.

As we, the Client and I, move forward with the work, I find that it helps also the bonding process of the work, and increases the therapeutic connection to the Client.

It gives the people I work with an understanding that I'm partially aware of where they are, even if I don't understand totally where they are. It also gives the focus of our work a much deeper and quicker connection.

I have people that say to me things like, 'I've told you so much more that I have ever told anyone else'. They also say, 'I don't understand why I feel so calm, why I feel so still, why I'm able to talk about these things with you'.

That is my view of 'In the Now' and hopefully it makes sense when you read this. That that would be helpful to you to understand a different way of seeing things that could make you more connected, more a part of and more immersed in.

Chapter 12
What and Why

Shortly after starting my new career as a Counsellor I became aware that the issues I was dealing with were more behavioural aspects that the Clients were bringing to look at or change. When I started the Counselling contract the Clients would say that they wanted to resolve this or stop that and as the work progressed I became more aware that in order to resolve the aspect that they were focussing on, I more often than was starting to explore why the behaviour happened, not the behaviour itself. As I grew in my experience and started working with deeper and more complex issues I began to challenge the Client's behaviour as a relationship to the actual reason for the behaviour, I call this way of seeing the Clients issues the "What and Why" concept.

This concept tries to make sense of how the Human conscious grapples with and understands the things we do and tries to bring conclusions to the issues and problems that they encounter in life. In order to understand the process, then we have to look at issues and problems from a different angle; we have to turn our normal process of rectifying things on its head to a great degree.

Think of it this way that we have two ways to look at everything we can do it the easy way and the hard way, the non-responsible way and the responsible way to work with things.

An example of this would be if your Teenage Son comes home and trashes their room, this behaviour is not the normal way you would expect them to react; you can then react in one of two ways. You can have a go at them and rant about them trashing their room and empathise they must clean their room up, maybe calling them names, belittling them, all of which will not normally bring about a resolution to the problem, you are saying this is all they're fault and they have to take responsibility for it, which on some level is true. This course of action is only likely to bring about more of the same behaviour or they may go quiet, internalising their issue and then start to distance them from the family or person that they see is giving them grief.

If you see this interaction in the "What and Why" concept, the behaviour would be the "What". "What's" are usually things that happen, things that the person does so the trashing of the room is a "What".
Keeping talking about the What will only lead to more What's or other displaced "What" reactions, it might change to them having a go at their siblings concentrating on other people's behaviour to offset theirs.

Possibly stealing things to bring attention to them in other ways, taking drugs etc. etc. If you then look at the Why you will see the things that are happening resulting in the What action, asking questions instead of attacking will offer an opportunity to gain insight into the Why. If you talk to the Teenager you may find that the What is just a way to get attention to talk about the Why which might be that they are being bullied at school, reacting to some change in the family, acting out because they find it extremely hard to talk about their feelings, The Why is always something that is happening to them, something they are experiencing or feeling.

If you chase them to stop the "What" then you will never find the Why and the What will just increase in severity or multiply to other more extreme and possibly dysfunctional What's.

The Why means that whatever the Teenager is experiencing could mean that you might have to take some responsibility for your part how their actions are making them react in the way they are doing. This is much harder to discuss and bring awareness and a positive outcome too, as it is easier to chastise the "What" than accept our part in the Why. In a wider context society as a whole chooses to work with the "What" than look at the Why, the What is easier as we can hold ourselves up as parables of virtue and not be connected to the What action which is happening.

If we look at the Why then we have to take responsibility in the part we play in the issue, we have to see ourselves as part of the problem and the What just as the persons reaction to our behaviour.

A common issue I see in my work is the one in which Adults are unfortunately divorcing and the fallout of that is usually a very dramatic change in the behaviour of any of the other people in the family who are caught up in this whirlpool of emotions. The Adults who are divorcing normally react to the other peoples behaviours without exploring them and the feelings behind them, due to the fact that the Adults don't want to look at the persons feelings as they cannot cope with how their actions are resulting in that person's behaviour. I don't blame the Adults in this process as they would find it hard to explore their feelings with others in the family when they themselves cannot cope with their own feelings.

In order to solve things please look at the Why not the "What", then you will find other peoples behaviours easier to resolve, they don't then become embedded in that person's life. See the person exhibiting the "What" as just someone who is trying to open up conversations with others to solve the "Why" issue rather than that person who is adding to or making the issue worse. See them as spearheading a resolution to the issue, a rescuer, not as the problem. Although our ownership of the "Why" feelings to the "What" problem will initially be harder.

Humans can only experience a limited amount of "Why" feelings were as we can utilise a never ending amount of "What" reactions.

You will see lots of examples of societies view in deflecting from going anywhere near taking responsibility for why people do what they do. The very aspect of being in the human race is not to take responsibility if we can avoid it. Look at Government proposals they will identify a need and then make some representation forward to help to overcome it, i.e. throw money at it to show we are doing something, an action the "What" then we do not have to look at the "Why"

If you take the work they do with people who might be addicted to drink or drugs, they demonise the action, taking drugs, but never resource the reason the "Why" people would take the drugs in the first place. Very little resources are in place to get to the reason as in this the people would have to take their responsibility for the action. People don't usually take drugs because they like them they usually take them to get away from the life they are having or have had. I their life was so bad then at some point us, society, would have to ask what is it we are doing, or not doing, to make that person not want to be in this reality world, being in this non reality world instead. That would take a huge leap for it to happen and all of us would have to take our individual responsibility in the process of that persons need to be out of it.

Onwards

My work as a Counsellor is very varied I like it that way as it stimulates and energises me. I have always liked working with different combinations of people and I am constantly interested in the vast array of issues they bring to the counselling process. I see the work as something more of a vocation than a job, even though I make a living from it. It constantly amazes me how when I started Counselling I would have an individual Client then it's like the scenario with London busses, lots more Client's come along and you acquire more Client's with very similar issues. It's strange how this works almost like they know you are working with the issues and that you're achieving experience and expertise with what is being worked with so you're the right person for the job, it's amazing.

It sometimes seems that to specialise with an issue you get lots of practice with similar clients that book the appointments. My work over the years has developed and grown in complexity and variety and I have worked in many different settings, this has helped me, not only to advance the work I do, but also to engage with different organisations and different ways of working. This diversity of work is what keeps me going and keeps me interested.

I would say to anyone thinking of taking up counselling as an occupation that whatever aspects of human behaviour you are looking to work with make sure that you are interested in the client group and the issues they bring and that it gives you satisfaction and contentment in what you do.

Be aware of your own issues and try as much as possible not to work with any client group in which you don't feel comfortable or that you have not processed any unresolved issues or feelings which you are working with that connect with your own life. As I constantly grow and develop my practice in all sorts of ways I feel humbled that people over the years have been able to be so honest with me and that they have allowed me to help them to come to terms with the things that have gone wrong in their lives. Exploring ways in which to move on or change the things they wish to change in their worlds.

The exploration and harnessing of the Intuitive work I do is very exciting as I develop the process and teach other people to work with this futuristic and valuable enhancing tool which is suitable for any therapy.

It is taking me on a journey of discovery not only for myself but also for my new Clients that they feel is helpful and beneficial to help them in moving them on and to have better lives.

It feels such a natural way to work and as I assimilate it more into the work I do it's just more comfortable.

I have no idea where I will end up and what I will experience on the way but I wake up every day with a happiness and desire to explore what life throws at me and honestly I can say that I still find life exciting and fulfilling and look to each new day with a freshness and pride in the work I do.

Long may it continue?

Tools

Time Out

This is just a phrase which we use to help people understand the process.

It enables people to stop arguments, as long as it is honoured and respected.

The process is to use a phrase known to both parties which signals to them that the emotion in the room is escalating and it is time to call a halt, Time Out, before a full blown argument ensues. This phrase can be Time Out itself, or any phrase which works for the couple which is not in their ordinary, everyday language and cannot be confused for ordinary speech. This phrase is known to both of them, and is established in advance once they begin working with controlling their destructive emotions.

They also have to agree a time span; this is the amount of time it would take each party to calm down, to bring their temper under control. Then as soon as one of the parties realises that the communication is going into an argument phase, they take the responsibility to call their word or phrase or 'Time Out' and the other party has to respect their decision.

They then move out of each other's face and space for the whole duration of the time they agreed to as being the length of time needed for them to bring their tempers under control.

Script Awareness tool

Use this tool in order to help you to look at the drives and scripts we are given from our significant others. It will help you to take control of your life and not have to follow their paths or teachings. Become aware of what it is you are doing that you would like to change or alter then follow this questioning process.

Script Origin Organisation or Person (Who gave you it)

Script Given (What message did they give you)

Reaction to Script (How does it drive you, make you do)

Positive (Do you like it and does the script help you)

Am I happy with it? (Its fine enjoy it)

Do I need to modify it? (What would I like it to be?)

Negative (It's not helpful)

Can it be changed? (Is it too painful to change it?)

What can it be changed to? (What do I want it to be?)

Am I happy with it? (Do I have to modify it?)

Enjoy the new aspect of you

You have a New script

Loss Cycle

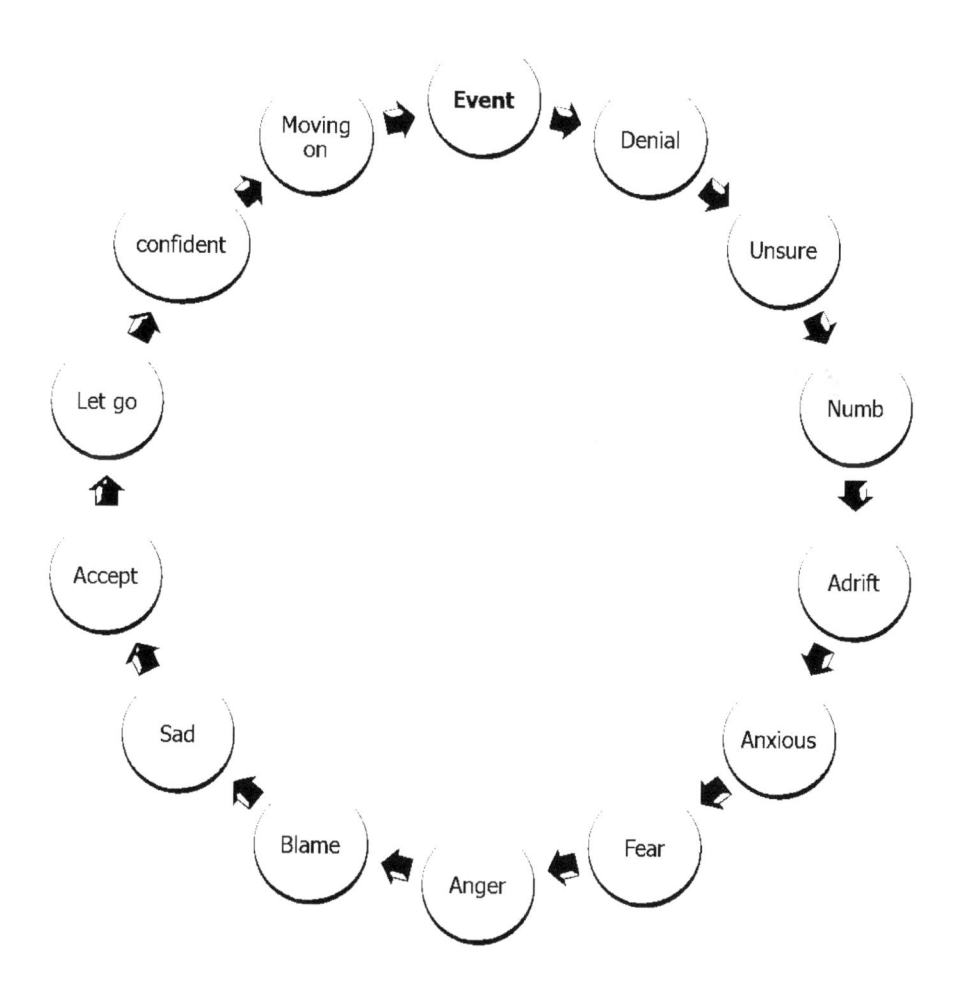

Event → Denial → Unsure → Numb → Adrift → Anxious → Fear → Anger → Blame → Sad → Accept → Let go → confident → Moving on → Event

The above process starts with the event and then you will experience some or more of these feelings as you journey through the cycle of Loss.

Don't worry as this is a process encounter the feeling and allow yourself to process it then your journey will be shorter and less painful.

Telling not Asking

Sometimes a person can 'Tell' another person their opinion, what to do, what to think, believing (in error) that they are communicating. In fact they are being overbearing, or controlling or even belligerent, and don't understand why the person they are 'Telling' reacts badly. Telling is usually the result of poor self-esteem, it is easier for the person to take the 'I know, I'm in charge' position than to Ask, enquire, be vulnerable to hearing an answer they may not like. They think they have 'fixed' the situation; this is their perception, they are doubly hurt to find they have made it all worse.

We all perceive the world in a unique and individual way, this perception is developed by the things that have been shown to us, our peer group, family, learning, or by things that have happened to us, our experiences. This perception is fine for us, it usually keeps us safe and secure, but when we use it to 'help others' by telling them we find it seldom creates the right environment of helping as others can perceive this as interfering or controlling. Our perception is only that, a perception, it will never be the other person's reality; in order to find the real reality we need to ask them what their perception is also. Usually when our partners or the people close to us are sounding off about work or friends or things that don't connect you and them, they usually just want someone to listen to their gripes or moans.

Not to actively fix anything, as usually these things cannot be fixed, but we believe in order to help the other person we need to fix it, be the rescuer, Tell them how to solve it. This is more often than not a Male trait but can be part of the female trait as well.

This "Telling not Asking" process does not validate or respect the other person's position. Sometimes it can give the other person the feeling of "what is the point in telling you what I have to say as this is not what you want to hear from me?", so they reduce the communication between the both of you, adding distance between the two of you. It also can dramatically close the dialogue between you, if they think that a particular situation is off limits due to this Telling then all that connects to the situation will also be withdrawn from the communication possibilities between the both of you and undoubtedly make it worse. This reduction will not only effect that situation but any other situation that connects not only the circumstances but also the feelings.

Therefore it is much better to "Ask than Tell", to find the reality and not the perception, as the perception is always a possible and never an actual.
If you follow this rule of "Asking not Telling", this opens dialogue, creates a joining and reinforces the relationship between you both.

Asking creates harmony and clarity; Telling usually creates disharmony and division.

No One is an Island

We all need others to help make our life complete as Humans are generally a socially engaged species. The type of person or groups we need is obviously different for each individual. The best fit of group to the individual person would be one that is stimulating, healthy, respectful, productive and engaging. The problem with some people' socialising is that they find that by engaging with others they sometimes find they are the round peg in the square hole. This usually applies more when we have been in a long term relationship and not necessarily engaging with others, that we have chosen, we sometimes find we cannot venture outside our close connections or our partners close connections, possibly family or old friends. This trying to engage with new connections means that we might have to increase our confidence or think that we deserve this aspect of thinking and concentrating on just our self's needs. So try not to just stumble through this engaging process of accepting others that we know and there groupings and start to think about what your individual needs are and where you might find those needs being met. This process is best if you can write it down, there is something about achieving clarity by seeing it written on paper. Write down the things that do all the things I talked about above: Stimulating: write down the things that you find stimulating.

Healthy: what would you like in your life to make you feel healthy, physically, mentally or emotionally?
Respectful: Where would you feel that others treat you with respect?
Productive: What would help you extend or improve yourself?
Engaging: where would you go to feel that others would allow you to be you the individual?

Use the re-evaluating tool, which you can find on the site when you join it, to help you here and always check to see if the choices you have made still give you the things you require and if you find they or you have moved or altered update your needs and re-evaluate your life again.

Re-evaluating process

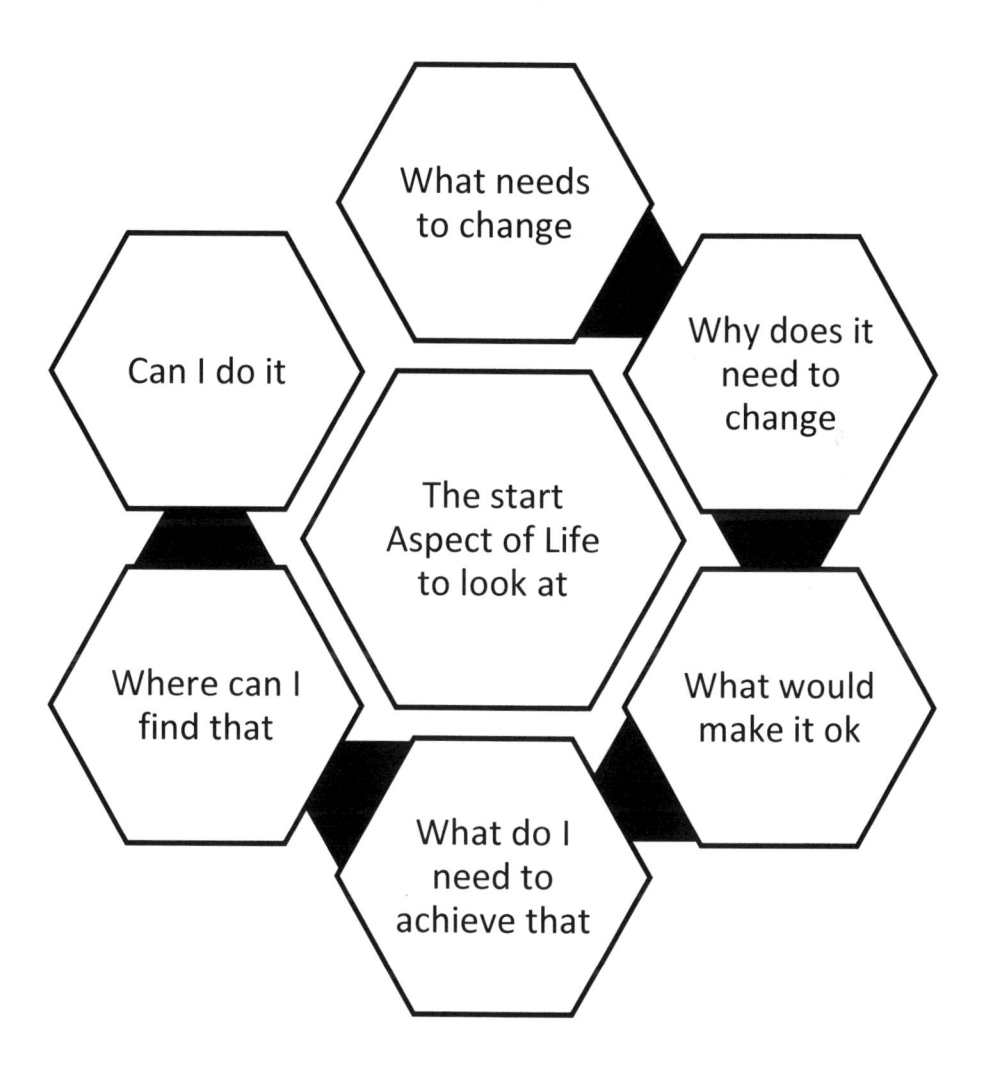

- What needs to change
- Can I do it
- Why does it need to change
- The start Aspect of Life to look at
- Where can I find that
- What would make it ok
- What do I need to achieve that

Use the above diagram to help to clarify your options and thought process in order to get what you want from a particular situation.

Are you in charge of your life?

This diagram will help you to understand whether you are in control of things within your life or whether someone or something else is. The red print is just an example to show you how to use the diagram you may want to use different headings. The headings on the left hand column, aspect of your life, is to help you to focus in on that particular area of your life, this can help you to clarify and separate it within all the other things you do. This mind prompt tool helps you to take away the busyness of your life, and all the other things which get in the way for you to see and think about things clearly. Writing things down makes them real, as in our heads we can choose to dismiss or minimise things that are happening to us, writing anything down to make sense of it is helpful.

Aspect of your life	Breakdown of Aspect	Do I think I'm in Control Is it ok	Do I think I'm Being Controlled By Who	Change required If any
Time	Health	Not always	Sometimes by my family's needs	More time for doing healthy activities
	Career Housework Reading Walking			
Emotions				
Money				
Movements				
Health				

Power Wall to enhance change

Positive feedback	Recorded Sucessses
Position this somewhere you	
Vision place	Negative views of Self

In the positive feedback box: Ask four to six supportive people to give you their views of the positive aspects of your character and write them here.

In the Recorded Successes Box: Place here any written feedback of your successes this could be exams, tests, achievements or any feedback from an accredited source.

In the vision Box: Place pictures here to invest in your future. They could be things you want to own or things you want to achieve in your life.

In the negative views of self Box: Write all the negative aspects of your characteristics here. If the views of your supportive people in the positive feedback box oppose your views you have to remove and destroy your views.

The above tool will help you to build your confidence and self-esteem. Draw the power wall on a large piece of paper and place it somewhere that you will be able to see on a regular basis. The brain takes everything in and remembers it even if we do not pay particular attention to things so a drip drip effect occurs to see you differently. It builds your power and hence your confidence.

Fears and challenging them

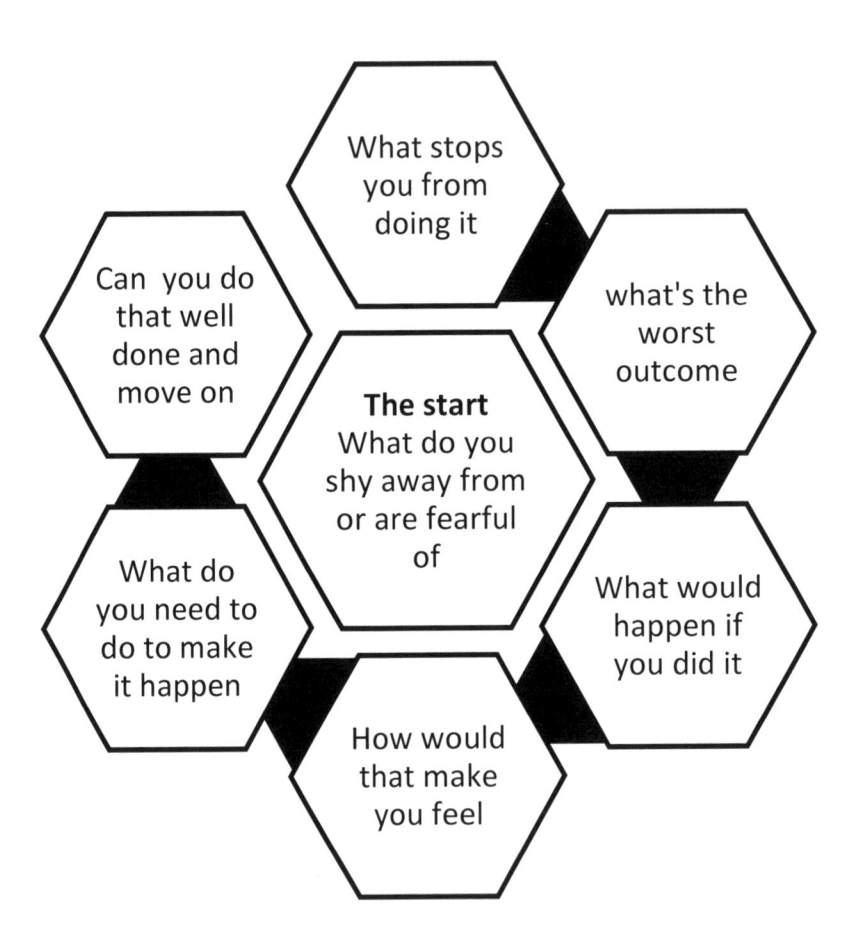

- **The start** — What do you shy away from or are fearful of
- What stops you from doing it
- what's the worst outcome
- What would happen if you did it
- How would that make you feel
- What do you need to do to make it happen
- Can you do that well done and move on

If not and it was too fearful go back to the start and re-evaluate it from what you have learnt about the fear.

Using fear constructively

If we use fear as a negative we are more likely to retract from it then if we use it as a positive process. If we can use it as a positive process it will make us aware just that there is something different or new coming into our lives, this helps us to see it just as something we have never done before, something new, a challenge and then we can grow from it. I now use fear as a positive enforcement that something new is happening and grasp it for change and movement; yes sometimes it will not be as good an experience as we would like or we perceived it to be. Exceptional growth as I have found comes more from hard experiences than soft easy ones. So if you want to grow then you have to embrace both aspects whether perceived to be good and bad. Use the following mantra.

Fear
Is the step Just before
Awareness

Awareness
Is the step just before
Acceptance

Acceptance means you have moved on
Until you find the next fear

Then you go through the process again

This way of working as I have said can be slightly scary but if you look at it from the point of view above.

It's a bit like taking a rollercoaster ride for the first time, and the fear you would naturally feel as the rides queue gets shorter and the time to go on the ride gets nearer your anxiety naturally increases. Now when you're on the ride there is a feeling of being out of control, the ride is in charge of you, you are strapped in and cannot get out. You have to follow the rides course and whilst the ride is in action the feeling of highs and lows can be very scary. Once the ride has completed and you have experienced the whole of it, then if you went on the same ride again you would never feel as anxious again because you know the outcome. This is how I see life now, before I just did not realise that life was in control of me I was not in control of it, I thought I was in control, but in reality it was just a mirage I definitely wasn't.

The more of life's rides I go on, the more of life that I interact with, the calmer I get, then the more I get used to being with this out of control feeling and start to enjoy it for what it is. I know from experience myself that this way of being is not an easy one to maintain or live with but for me it works. I also realised, when I was going through this process of change, that in order to move on I could not hold onto things which had finished or the lessons which had been learnt.

In fairness I held onto situations which in reality should have ended a long time before they did. This letting go of the things that you cannot change and working with the things you can change is an enormous balancing act which I still get wrong today but endeavour to work at to get better at it.

Do not hold onto things which have passed their sell by date let them go before they make you ill?

Using alternative words

When we talk about situations in which we feel insecure we will say things we don't really mean, to ask questions but by using statements instead. I know this may sound confusing and strange but it is part of what humans do. It never gets the result that the person talking really wants but instead has the opposite reaction, so it's not really helpful at all and if you understand why we do this then you can choose to do something different in order to get you views across and ask the real questions you need the answers for.

An example of this would be if you were in your house and feeling insecure in your relationship and your partner wasn't listening to your needs, you may scream at them to leave, because you have lost all patience in getting your views heard, get out don't talk to me. You may physically push them to leave, verbally push them away. Most people don't really want that to happen most people would like that partner to show them that they are important to them, love them and would like to support them. We want them to say no I'm staying because I love you; I want to support and validate you. Instead of us being able to be honest with them and saying what we mean, I really need you, want you to keep me safe, we push them away. This way of communicating does not help but just confuses everyone and usually makes things worse.

The easiest and best way of communicating to someone is to be as honest as you can be, don't allow you insecurity to take control of your words and always say what you mean. The way to communicate your feelings or thoughts more effectively is to use I statements.
I statements mean that you own your communication; you speak from your own position and you never blame the other person.

An example of this in relation to the above example could be that you would say "I don't like it when I cannot feel heard and that makes me feel as though I am not connected to you. It makes me feel insecure and not valued when we argue and that just feels so horrible. I would love us to be able to talk calmly and for me be able to tell you how I really feel about our relationship. I want us to be closer and I want to really show you how much I care but I find it really hard to do this when I feel as though I am not important enough to be listened to.

This way of communicating, using I statements would normally bring people closer make your relationship partner more emotionally connected to you and allow them to show their feelings more easily towards you.
It's a much better process than arguing and achieves clarity, honesty and closeness.

Cycle of Insecure Talking

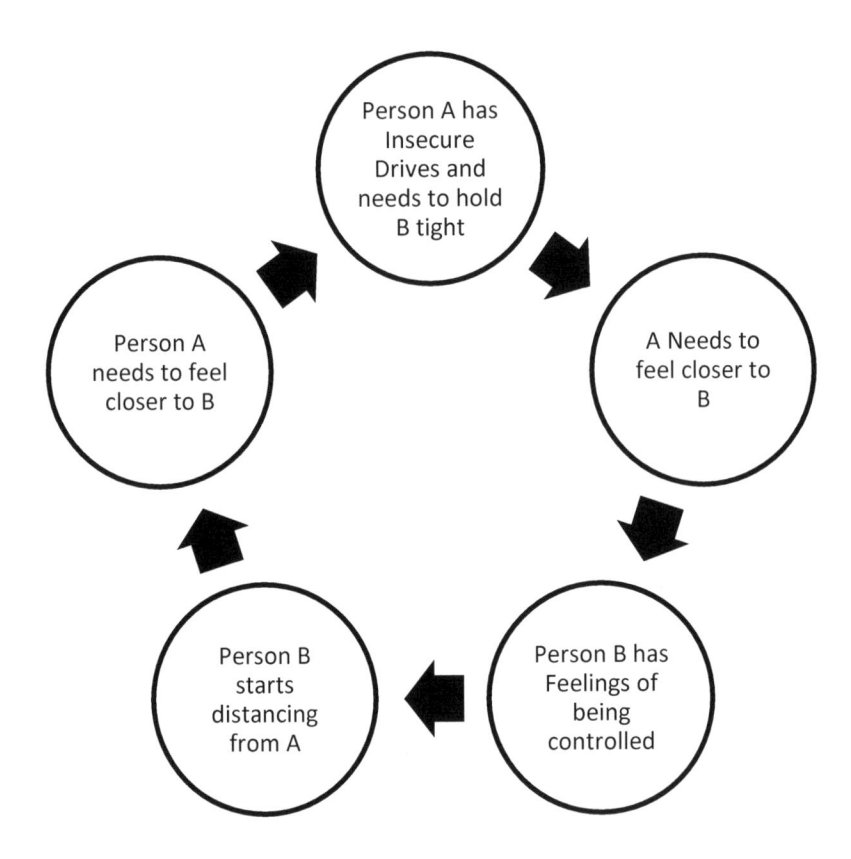

```
        Person A has
        Insecure
        Drives and
        needs to hold
        B tight

Person A                          A Needs to
needs to feel                     feel closer to
closer to B                       B

        Person B                  Person B has
        starts                    Feelings of
        distancing                being
        from A                    controlled
```

In this process A Needy uses pushing or demanding language to see if B wants them (B) Dismisses (A's) needs as they feel pushed A pushes harder so that B cannot do anything other than strongly verbally or physically react this results in stronger negative communication, which brings A closer but B will possibly feel used with repressed negative feelings. But as A's insecure needs can never be fully filled by B or any other person the drives return. The cycle will increase in intensity and frequency to facilitate A's increasing need to satisfy their internal insecurity.

Pebble in the pond process

Negative feelings are externalised and start transferring the ripple effect outwards on to others. Other people get those feelings react to them

When your emotions ripple out to others they will feel them and react accordingly. An example could be that you are annoyed and then catch a bus, the Driver asks you for your fare and you snap at him for no reason. The Driver then passes your negative emotion on to the next passenger and so on the ripp grows but sometimes in a diluted way. It's best to sort out your issues with the original person and not pass the ripple on to others.

Win Win process

When we want to achieve something positive with another person then we have to use a "win win" solution to achieve our aims. If the other person sees something positive for them in the agreement that they have achieved, as well as us, then they are more likely to accept it. So as in all negotiation's we need to establish a "win win" process. If one party just says they are ok with the outcome, either to pacify the other person or just to stop possible conflict then that will not really work. This person would then store their feelings of compliance and it would eventually get in the way of satisfaction with the end result. So in any compromise situation both parties need to be honest and be able to be completely happy with the outcome. Try to show the other person that they also win in this process and you will get the right long term result for both of you. In order to do this you need to find they're position and aims so you can structure the end result to include them and then you will have a constructive and long term solution to the relationship that you are undertaking with them. Negotiation is always better than manipulation.

I have a saying if you always do what you have always done; you always get what you have always got. Stop going round in the same circle and make a change to make a different circle.

Challenging Life Scripts

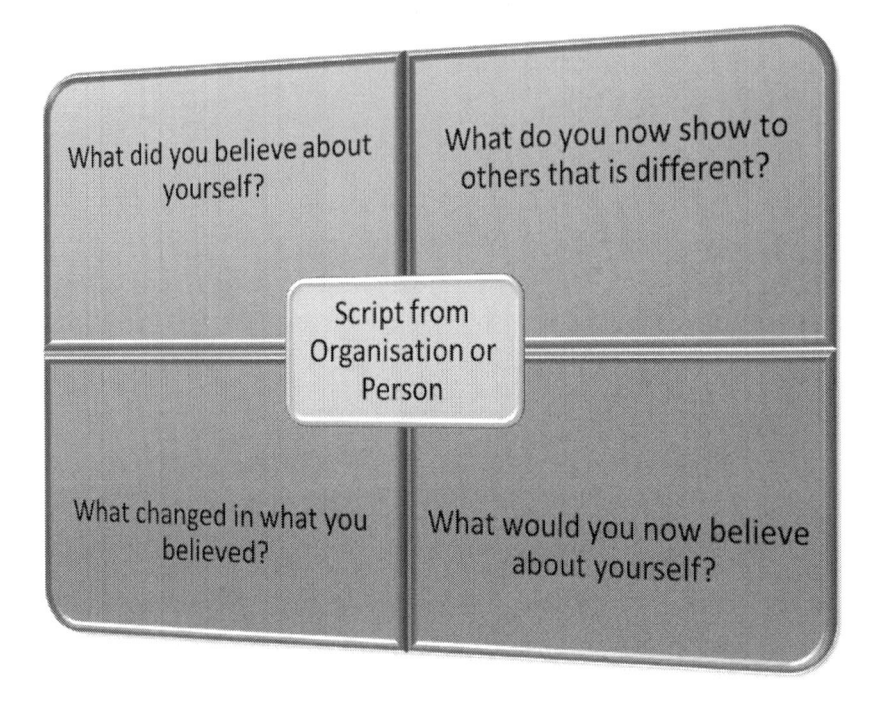

What did you believe about yourself?	What do you now show to others that is different?
Script from Organisation or Person	
What changed in what you believed?	What would you now believe about yourself?

Use the above tool to help you to look at your individual scripts take the origin of the scrip and example would be. The world outside is a scary place that you should not engage with. This script might make it hard for you to engage with new situations throughout your life. Once you are aware that you are being limited by this script and would like to change it then use the above tool to help to redefine the script and build your own script.

Identifying and Changing Scripts

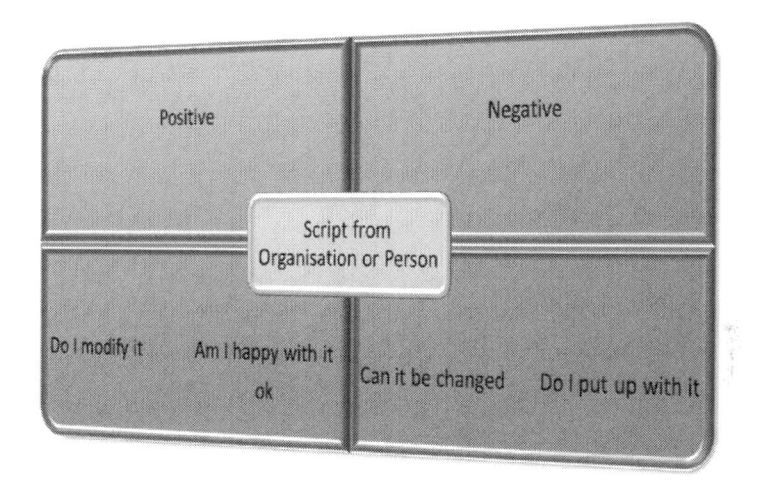

Positive	Negative
	Script from Organisation or Person
Do I modify it Am I happy with it ok	Can it be changed Do I put up with it

This results in:

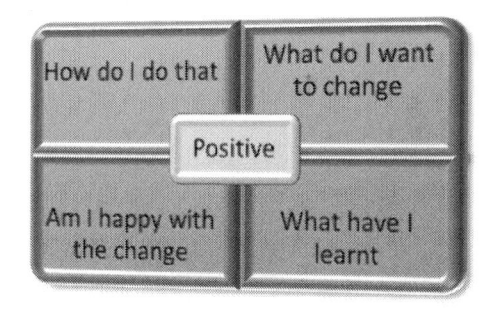

How do I do that	What do I want to change
	Positive
Am I happy with the change	What have I learnt

This results in:

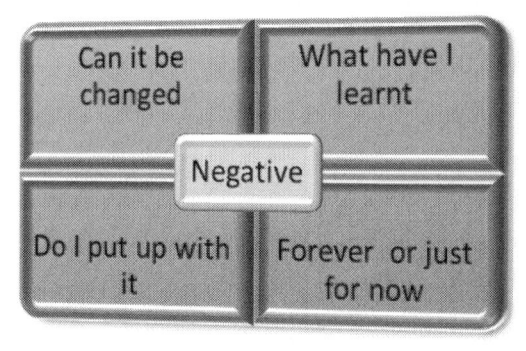

Can it be changed	What have I learnt
	Negative
Do I put up with it	Forever or just for now

Use the above tool to help to engage with possibly new ways to see yourself and what options you have. The questions used help you engage more fully with the process and shift your thoughts. They also help to engage with forward processes and not victim restrictions.

Co-Dependency

What is it?

There are many definitions used to talk about co-dependency today. The original concept of co-dependency was developed to sometimes acknowledge the responses and behaviours people develop from living with an alcoholic or substance abuser. A number of attributes can be developed as a result of those conditions.

However, over the years, the term co-dependency has expanded into a definition which describes a dysfunctional pattern of living and problem solving developed during childhood by family rules.

One of many definitions of co-dependency is: - inability for a person to develop behaviours which can get their needs met, and/or compulsive behaviours learned by family members in order to survive in a family which is experiencing great emotional pain and stress.

As adults, co-dependent people have a greater tendency to get involved in "toxic relationships", in other words with people who are perhaps unreliable, emotionally unavailable, or needy people. And the co-dependent person tries to provide and control everything within the relationship without addressing their own needs or desires; setting themselves up for continued un-fulfilment. This initially can be the basis of a relationship which can be very fulfilling for both parties.

Even when a co-dependent person encounters someone with healthy boundaries, the co-dependent person still operates in their own system; they're not likely to get too involved with people who have healthy boundaries. This of course creates problems that continue to recycle; if co-dependent people can't get involved with people who have healthy behaviours and coping skills, then the problems can continue into each new relationship they connect with. These relationships do not have to be intimate ones friends can be co-dependant relationships but the relationships will be sometimes exhausting and claustrophobic.

How do I know if I'm co-dependent?
Generally, if you're feeling unfulfilled consistently in relationships, you tend to be indirect, don't assert yourself when you have a need to, if you're able to recognize you don't play a part in the relationship as much as others, or that other people point out you could be more involved in getting your needs met, that the relationship is un-balanced. Things like this can indicate you're co-dependent.

What are some of the symptoms?
- Controlling behaviour
- Distrust
- Perfectionism
- Avoidance of feelings
- Intimacy problems
- Caretaking behaviour
- Heightened awareness for potential threat/danger
- Physical illness related to stress

Isn't everyone co-dependent?
To a degree yes possibly as we all need others to be connected to. There are some natural and healthy behaviour mothers do with children that can look like co-dependency, as both need each other. Are people mutually interdependent on each other? Yes. There is perhaps a continuum of co-dependency that most people might fall into. Maybe this continuum exists because so many people are taught not to be assertive at a young age as this can be seen as selfish, or to ask directly for their needs to be met? We probably can't say though that everyone is co-dependent. Many people probably don't feel fulfilled because of other things going on in their systems at large.

General rules set-up within families that may cause co-dependency could include:
- It's not okay to talk about your problems
- Feelings should not be expressed openly; keep your feelings to yourself
- Communication is best if indirect; one person acts as messenger between two others; known in therapy as 'triangulation'
- Be strong, good, right, and perfect, something that can never be achieved
- Make us proud of you, beyond realistic expectations
- Don't be selfish
- Do as I say not as I do
- It's not okay to play or be playful with others
- Don't rock the boat keep your views to yourself?

Many families have one or more of these rules in place within the family system. These kinds of rules can constrict us and strain our free and healthy development of our self-esteem, and coping strategies.
As a result, children can develop non-helpful behaviour characteristics, problems in solving issues in life, and negative reactions to situations in their adult life.

As I said earlier we are all too some extent dependant on others and that is not necessarily a problem.

"Nothing is a problem unless it's a problem"
Sometimes relationships can thrive on this type of interaction and will be fine until one of the participants wants to grow, change or develop. This then threatens the relationship rules and hence can cause friction or a feeling of being restricted which will stress the relationship.

If both parties can allow the other to grow and not feel threatened or insecure then harmony can rein. If the co-dependency is a sub-conscious response the likely hood is that it will not be worked with but reacted to. If you can use the script tools above you can then change the outcome to be a conscious process with choices.

The level of masks we show

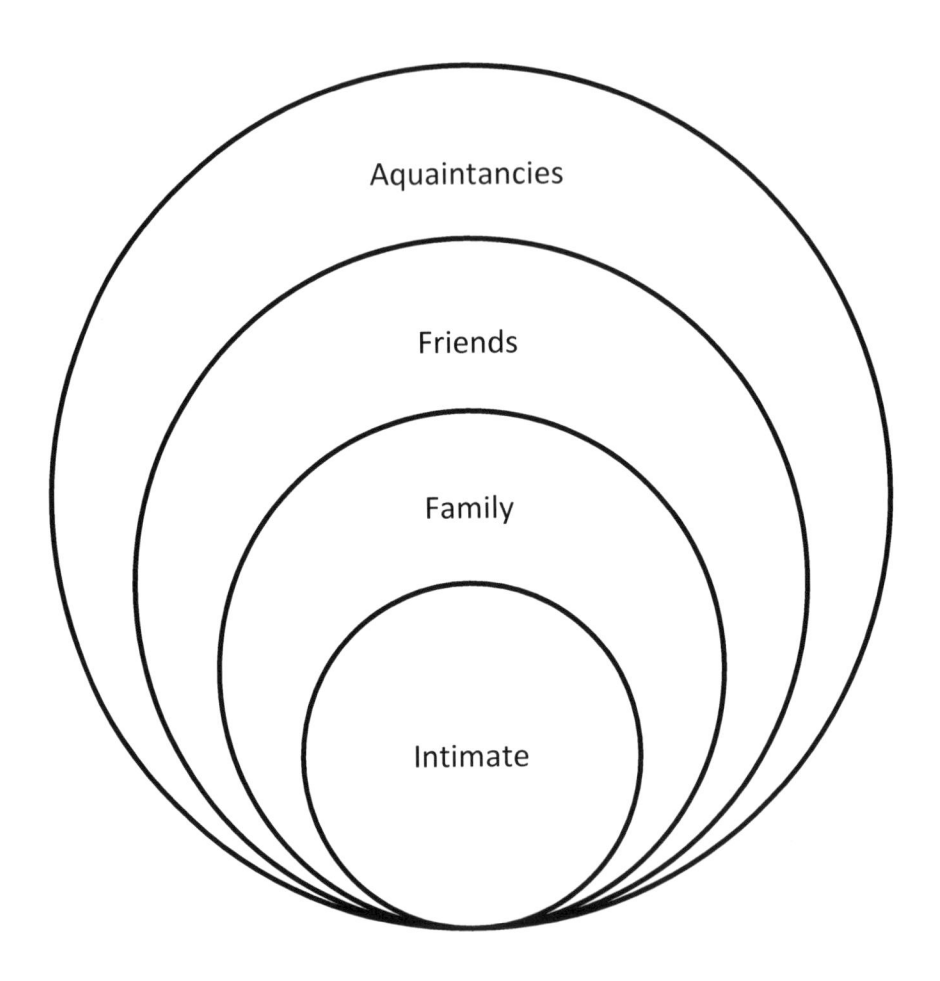

- Aquaintancies
- Friends
- Family
- Intimate

These are not hard boundaries and some people will sometimes move between the boundary lines dependant on how your relationships change. The titles are only examples you may want to use different ones or have more of them.

Plot on the graph where your individual people fit your different mask

Perception and reality

All Human Beings work from a historical premise, that what we know, have learnt and understand, informs our interactions within our world today, our "Perception" is our "Reality". This way of understanding the way the world works is sometimes an issue for partners because all of our perspectives are as individual as ourselves; even twins will have a completely different way of perceiving and interacting within their world. This difference is usually initially the reason why things break down in relationships; we cannot seem to understand the other person's point of view, because we have no experience or knowledge to understand it. So we perceive it the way we think it is and we will always get it wrong, no-one's perception will ever be "The Reality" as we all have different views so no one view will ever be the same as ours, it will be our reality but not necessarily "The Reality." We cannot easily change our perception/reality unless we can challenge it nor have it challenged in a way that does not threaten us then we will be able to modify it.

When we connect with another human being, we have a relationship, whether it is at work, home, friend or sexual partner, in this relationship we communicate to understand each other, so we may find a common reality, the reality in-between our individual realities, a shared view.

This works fine as long as we keep checking it out and reframing it as things change, our reality is really always changing, in a subtle way, as the experiences we are having are always changing us, minute on minute, day on day. It's when we stop checking out the other persons perception, or the communication between us breaks down, we tend then to start using our individual perception to understand what is happening instead of asking for the other person's perception as well, so we have a piece missing to inform us of what is really going on. When we do this it infers to the other person that we know how they feel, what they want, usually in statements like "You feel I am" or "I think you are" - when we do this we are using our perception to understand their reality. So the golden rules are "Don't assume, talk" "Don't think ask".

Using the Ask don't Tell chapter will help, then you will always be working with The Shared Reality not just your reality.

Systems and how they interconnect

You are at the centre of the system everything originates from you

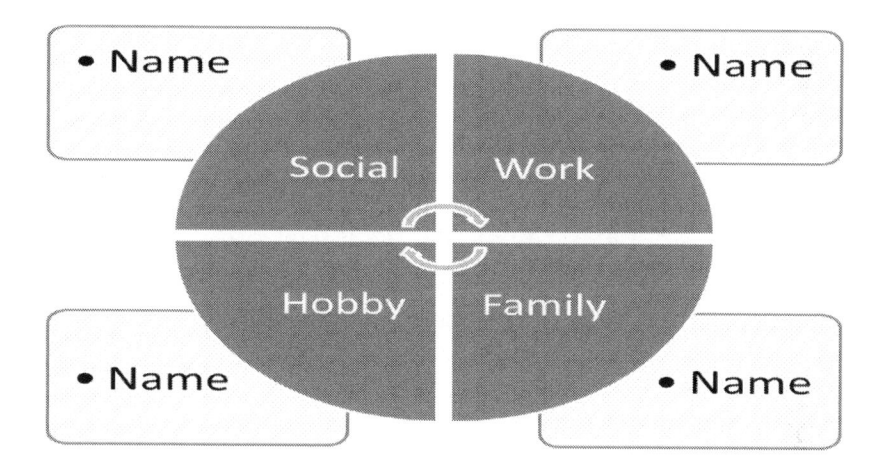

- Name

- Name

Social | Work

Hobby | Family

- Name

- Name

Use this guide to help you plot your interconnections and the systems that you revolve in and around and the ones in which you share your life. Find how close you are and how those systems affect you and make choices to change the inter-connections if you want to. Remember the system you are in needs you and therefore you have the power.

Talking Time

Talking time is a structured process I use to enable people, whose communication has broken down, to re-connect and start to feel they are heard again. What you need to do is to have a constructed space of time with no interruptions, no less than half an hour and no more than an hour, as this exercise can be quite emotionally tiring.
These sessions should be a least once but no more than twice a week. In this constructed time space you find some way of timing yourselves, egg timer or watch, for example, for about 3-4 minutes. You can throw a dice or toss a coin to see who goes first then when the first person has their go they can talk about anything, but from their own perspective they own the conversation, speaking from the I.

The other person just actively listens intently to what is being said; they do not interrupt or input anything into the exploration that the person is undertaking. This does two things it allows someone to talk with no interruptions and also it allows them to feel truly heard. The one thing I hear most from couples and families is that they don't feel heard when they talk. When the first timed session has elapsed then the other person can start their exploration about how they feel about what they have heard or they are able to move the conversation on to any other subject they want to explore.

But always remembering that they own the exploration, they talk from the I position.

This time is not a process of blame or defending your-self but a space that each person can start again to understand the others feelings or thoughts it respects and validates each person and helps to re-engage in a positive constructive way. I find most people who interact with this process initially feel stifled in their communication but then they settle into it and find it enormously beneficial, stick with it.

Working with Affairs

Pointers for the hurt Partner

Here are some pointers which might be beneficial on your road to recovery:

Healing may take longer than you imagine possibly from 1 to 2 years to build the trust.

Don't try to side step your feelings. Find a safe way to share them, ideally with your partner so you can work through them. Try to look at your responsibility in the breakdown of the relationship. It's rare that a relationship breaks down purely due to one partner's reaction.

Try to understand that your partner is in a totally different emotional place to you and that does not mean they are not sorry or that they do not love you.

It's totally normal to have extremes of emotional outbursts, it does not help to just vent these to your partner, doing this just makes it unsafe for them to listen or help you come to terms with what has happened. Instead try to diary some time to talk openly and honestly with them in a constructive not destructive way, Counselling will help enormously with this process. The talking time tool can help you with this.

If you feel that you have to vent or dump these feelings then maybe this would be better done in front of the Counsellor so they can control the sessions so your partner can actively listen to them in a safe constructive way. If you are not seeing a Counsellor then the Letters tool will help you.

Try not to fill all the time you spend together with venting or dumping your feelings, give some space for the healing process to build the relationship again. The Quality time tool will help with this.

It's critical that you get the answers to your questions from your partner about the affair, this will abate the feelings and emotions easier, even if the same questions are asked time and time again, it's a process of building the trust again between you both.

Ask for clarification and reassurance as to what the affair meant, providing the time as and when you need it, which is safe and not filled with interruptions from others. The perception and reality tool will help here.

Try not to use negative communication structures as this will only build the arguments and not generate a useful understanding of the issues around the affair. A negative communication is one which when you talk you can see a pointy finger aiming at the partner, they will only retaliate to secure their position which will not aid your need to understand.

The arguments tool and communication information will help you here.

Don't make any hasty decisions about the future; an informed choice is always better than a reactionary one. Informed choices we can live with reactionary ones we will always regret or question at some point.

Take personal responsibility for your own healing, try to understand what you require from your partner and then ask for it in a constructive way.
Receive the information that your partner gives you with understanding it may also be hard for them to verbalise things to you as they will also possibly be confused as to why they did what they did.

Pointers for the unfaithful Partner

Here are some pointers that will help both you and your partner's journey through this situation.

You will possibly have had more time to deal with the awareness of your affair. It is therefore imperative that you are absolutely patient with your partner, especially at the start of this process. The longer that you have deceived the partner the more time it is likely they will need to build the trust again between you. Remember an affair does not have to have had a physical connection; normally it's the lies and deceit which are the issues which cause the problems.

The following aspects usually give the best conditions for building the trust between you again.
a) The sooner you stop all contact with the other party in the affair the better.
b) Tell the complete truth even if previously you have not, you never know what they may know.
c) Tell the complete truth even if it hurts your partner, as being hurt now is better than finding out later, this will cause even more distrust in the future and just like snakes and ladders you will end up back at the very beginning.
d) Realise that your partner is in a much different place to yourself, they will need to ask many questions, maybe the same question time and time again, which to you will be frustrating, but is necessary to enable them to move on.
e) Try to understand why you had the affair as this will help your partner know whether in the future, if similar things are happening in the relationship that the relationship could possibly be breaking down again. This searching for an answer will also show your partner that you are trying to help both of you through this very painful process.
f) Tell your partner also how you feel and support them in the process of building the trust between you. Never say you will be anything you cannot be, even if you think It's not what they want to hear, e.g. don't tell them you can be somewhere at a specific time, or do a specific thing for them, if you know that might not be possible, be honest in all things.

g) Be supportive and say SORRY for what has happened, initially this may not be accepted but still say it, it will eventually get through.
h) Expect emotional outbursts from your partner- they will be devastated and the pendulum of pain will swing erratically from ok to not ok, happy to sad, calm to explosive, sometimes from minute to minute. Be kind, patient, non-defensive and above all else honest.

It's normal for you to have a sense of loss around the affair, usually it's because that person took an interest in you or what you had to say, and it will be hard to talk to your partner at this moment. Don't expect your partner to listen to this at first, as you were sharing things with a third party that should have been kept within the relationship with you partner. You may feel confused as to your feelings, so it's good to clarify what they are, with your partner if possible, as this may shed light on why the affair happened, or with a counsellor on your own. Praise your partner's interactions in trying to understand with you what went wrong and why. Support their feelings and validate their courage in going through this process, which is going to be painful and possibly humiliating for them.

Pointers to Building the future Relationship

Understand and explore the reasons for the affair in a safe and nurturing environment.

Support and validate each other's feelings, even though you may not understand them.
Spend some quality time together, without talking about the affair, to build the relationship again together.
Realise that the old relationship is over; if it was ok then you would not be in this position now.
Build a new relationship by identifying each other's current needs and fulfilling them, give the relationship an MOT test.
Be honest with each other and tell each other how you feel on a regular basis without blaming.
Understand that you two are the most important features in the relationship, without you two being ok then the rest falls down.
Re-establish a physical bond, not necessarily sexual, hugs, kisses, holding hands; etc. may be all that is available at this time.

Above all be patient, Rome was not built in a Day, you are looking to build the new relationship stronger and better than it was before - this will take time.

This is not an exhaustive list of things which unmake or make a relationship
But a selection of the most common features that happen when trust is an issue within a relationship. You may find more reactions or interactions and as such use it as a possible pointer not a definite direction.

In my experience there are only three reasons why someone would have an affair

1) They do not want to be with their current partner they want to be with the new person. (I don't normally see the unfaithful person but can sometimes see and help the deserted one).
2) They want to push a big button that tells the partner that they are hurting and they don't know how to say that.
3) They are trying to find something which they need that is not being supplied or fulfilled in their current relationship.

It can be also a combination of 2 and 3 sometimes

Quality Time

Spending time with loved ones when relationships have become tired or routine can be awkward. This tool will help you to change the routine and increase the connection between you both. It also helps where couples have fallen into the trap of one partner always taking responsibility for making things happen or one of them needing to be in control.

Both partners have a container, a 'surprise jar', and they put 10 – 12 activities they would like to do outside of the home in their container, on slips of paper, which can be folded up to hide the contents, a real surprise. This needs to be something they want, not something they feel their partner would like, you can be selfish here. Then you plan a regular time frame of going out when you can find quality time together, the frequency of this time is whatever you feel is appropriate or achievable. This is time on your own, with no one else present.

You can then throw a dice, flip a coin, etc., to see who goes first. The one, who gets first go, picks one of the pieces of paper out of the other persons' container and takes full responsibility in making it happen. The other partner then just gets a treat, something they have asked for, alleviating the problem or worry of organising something which your partner may not like.

It is usually the case that if one partner does not treat the other it's because they have stopped trying too, due to a perception or fear of getting it wrong or it not being good enough.

This tool also validates the person having the surprise; however, it does not have to be a surprise, as some people like to know what they may need to wear for example.
The next planned outing time you just reverse the roles and the other partner picks out of the container and makes it happen for the other partner. You then alternate the process at every quality time session. This tool helps to bring difference and variety into the time spent together and can also be used for any children in the family allowing them also to have a container, (although you would have to sift and filter them that they are not all trips to Disney Land!)

Working with Grief

Grief is a terrible and alienating process, all of us respond to grief in different ways and it's hard to understand or cope with another person's grief process that is why it can be alienating and destructive.
The process of grief usually starts with denial, they will come back, they are not gone, sometimes waiting for the key in the door or the voice in the hall or on the telephone, in this time the person trying to come to terms with their loss will possibly put there life on hold and not do anything, shutting out reality, immersing themselves in a different world of hope, withdrawing from others close to them, that are also trying to come to terms with the loss, possibly arguing with the closest people to them, not accepting the reality that the person has gone. This can be a very destructive process and can separate families, friends and collective groups and would need a service like Cruise or an experienced Counsellor to help heal the void between them and others.

Sometimes the next stage is anger, which is very hard to process, you are not likely to want to be angry with the one you have just lost, but this is a natural part of the process even if it's just I'm angry at you going, why are you not here etc.

Again sometimes people can miss this part out and it will come back later on in another time or place, possibly at another moment of loss, which does not necessarily have to be losing someone but can be just losing a piece of paper or anything. If one person, the strong person in the family system, takes responsibility for the deceased person's arrangements then they may not go through the process of grief because they are too busy, but then the emotions of loss will have to be interacted with sometime in the future, occasionally many years later. The time it will take us all to go through this process of loss is different and there is no formula for it in this sense but the process is just that, it's a process and there will be a start, a during and a finish. Just be aware people need space and time to cope with loss and nothing is right or wrong but the best way of coping is to talk and be helped to interact with your emotions.

An example of this would be if someone close to you both had died and you both became stuck in your individual experience of grief, unable to talk or help each other through the process, it may then result in talking or connecting with any future aspect of loss being off limits between you.

For example, the loss of a job or a house, as this would need you both to re-connect with the original feelings of loss and that would also connect back to the current issue you are going through.

This connection and disconnection of feelings alienates us and divides us in lots of areas of our life and therefore also divides our communication process, as we are unable to voice the very things which need to be said. More than one person shouldering the responsibility of the organising will be very helpful as too share this responsibility would bring them together they would have to talk about the arrangements and share them this would help them to talk about the person who has gone and give rise to emotional bonding and sharing.

The main aspect of working with grief is that it cannot be rushed it has to be processed in a time that is suitable for the individual so a softly softly approach is paramount when working to help someone who is experiencing grief.

It does not matter how many times you have encountered loss in the pass each time it will be different, dependant on lots of variables, your relationship with the deceased, what else is going on for you at the time, your state of mind, how emotionally secure you are at the time, how you connect with others in the group etc. etc.

My flexible structure when working with grief is that first of all I check whether this is the right time for the Client to do the work, are they able to see that loss has taken place. It's no use working with someone who is in denial and forcing them to look at something that they don't want to look at; this would be an abusive act and stop any therapeutic work.

The current rational rule of thumb is that no grief work would be helpful before 4-6 months after the loss has occurred but as I have said each person is different.

If for example someone had lost a close family member and they had experienced a time between the loss and the body being found, possibly when the body had decomposed or did not look like the person they had lost. You would then maybe have to work with them on the fact that they're denial would stop them even contemplating that loss had taken place. So for me the first aspect of the work would be to check they're ready to accept that loss had actually happened and then to start moving them to a place where they could start to talk about that loss.
The next part of the work is to allow them to paint me a picture of the person, so I could know them, either with using photos or the deceased person's effects.

When you are doing this part of the counselling work great respect must be had for the items they have brought into the counselling room, handle them with reverence and respect never grab them wait for them to be given up, hold them softly and gently when you talk about them. You could slow down the handing over of the object so that you both are holding it at the same time whilst talking about it and the connection to the deceased person.

Being both physically connected to the item can help the discussion.

Once you have discussed an item then place it on a table or surface between you both don't put it away, as they might be upset that the item has been put out of sight, incurring another loss feeling. You may also need to come back to it later so keep it handy. Keep building the picture and allowing them to talk about their life with them, things they did, places they saw, their temperament trying to allow the positive and also the negative aspects of the person to be gently explored, as no person is a saint but they may initially try to paint them as one.

At the end of any session ask them if they would like to leave the items with you for safe keeping or whether they would like to take them home, this may give you an indication of the reaction about whether they are ready to let them go or not. If they do leave them with you then please, please, please take good care of them put them in a receptacle that reflects respect and security and lock them away. If they have a high reaction to the thought of them leaving the items with you then that will give you an indication of whether they are moving towards letting go. You are only looking for the reaction as an indication of how close they are to letting them go and also how they might trust you, you possibly are not trying to get them to leave the item with you at all.

You are just using the item as a tool to give you understanding. If they have no items to bring or they don't like the idea of using real effects from the deceased then you could use stones, drawings or other items to build the picture of the person and they're connection to the deceased.

Once you have got a real understanding of the person who has been lost and you feel that you know them as well as you could, and that the therapeutic bond with the client is strong then you can start slowly asking about their faults, the normality of the person.
Getting the Client to understand that they were not a saint and that may well lead to allowing the anger out and an emotional unleashing of feelings.

Once you have fully connected the Client to their feelings then you can look at allowing them to slowly start to let the person go, you may want to talk about carrying out some ritual, a symbolic passing or letting go, maybe allowing clothes to be given to a charity or a cremation or burial of something that they can connect with the deceased over, a letter to them or a picture or a balloon release, whatever works for them these are only ideas not absolutes, immediacy is a great tool here for the Counsellor.

Allow them to build their own ceremony in their unique way if you were working with two or more people, then you might want to build this ceremony between all parties with everyone giving something that connects them to the deceased. After the ceremony then have at least one more session, to allow the loss of the therapist connection on the journey that you have been on to be processed, see how far they have come build their strength in them that they have achieved this goal and that they have survived. It's important that they feel resilience to the work and journey so they might be better placed in the future to cope with loss, as this aspect of being a human being is something we will all experience and it is normal and healthy to do this.

Above all remember this journey is at the Clients pace and should never be rushed, feel their position and whether they are comfortable, apologise if you do go too far to quick and take responsibility for that, never let them feel that it's their fault something has not worked, modelling ownership and responsibility of an issue is an important part of any therapeutic work. Denial of responsibility never helps it only alienates.

The Way Forward to Seeking Change

Most people want to move forward in some direction in their life, the problems usually come when they need to change something to enable the forward movement to happen. Changing your life involves an initial need to change yourself; it can't be done just by trying to change the circumstances you find yourself in. Even if you have an outside influence which forces change upon you, such as illness or being made redundant, the change begins with 'I', not 'it'. This recognition often operates the "rabbit in the headlight" feeling, as if you are not able to do anything - just staying where you are through a feeling of fear, being judged and not supported or some other general insecurity.

Remember "Fear is an emotional reaction; it is there to remind you that you are doing something you have never tried before. Once you have interacted with your fear it will never feel as fearful again. Fear can only hold you in its power if you allow it to."

When we try to change our life's positions, whatever they are, we need to carefully think first about what we would like to change, this sounds silly as we may know what we want to change, but change is a process, do you know where the beginning, middle and end of the process is?

Is it accessible in a one hit format, or will there be many steps?

Are you already some way along those steps or are you starting from scratch? It might be, for instance, that you want to change your career, in order to do that you may need to retrain in some way, so the change you want will not be available until that retraining starts. In this case you need to break the required change down to its individual parts and then start changing those aspects first.

The problem with most changes is that the change you want to happen seems so big on its own that it can never happen, you can't even get started, so breaking it down into bite size chunks is more accessible and more productive. The small steps tool will help you here.

Another aspect of restriction to change is that the people around you may not be happy with that change, or that might be what you perceive, perception is usually not reality, only a partial aspect of it. It is the way we talk and communicate to the people around us, which results in whether they will help or hinder our path.
If the words we use or the way we say them communicates that we will change and move away from them.

They will usually feel insecure in our proposed change or how they perceive the effect of change, and how it might affect them and are unlikely to help us in the change.

Most people who find it hard to change will be people who give to others most of the time, they will usually find it hard to find time to look at or think about what they want for themselves. When they do, they will often withdraw from actual change because of their perception of other people's feelings or needs to that change.

When you talk to your significant others about your needs, do you state what you want calmly, confidently and positively, or do you say it sheepishly or matter-of-factly without conviction? For many of you that are reading this, it will be the latter, as people who can make change happen are usually more focused on their needs than others and see change as a natural part of life, which it is, they have no fear or trepidation about change.

People constantly ask me "when will I know I am on the right path", I can only tell you how it was for me. When you start on the right path for you, your journey of change, then you will find it moves without the need for lots of effort, if you are going forward in the right way it will be like "Swimming with the tide, everything will just flow,

When you are not going forward it will be like swimming against the tide".

The process of change is never an easy one for most people who care about others, the world etc. but the contentment, calm and "being at one with you" is always worth the effort. If you truly want to change then don't delay start at this moment and work the process, always remember, as a very wise person said, that every journey starts with a single step and each step gets you nearer your goal? So begin your change by starting to communicate your needs and eat that elephant one bite at a time.

Letters to release un-processed Emotions

When we store negative emotions, then we cannot keep them in all the time it would be like a pressure cooker being filled and filled till it cannot hold anymore being ready to explode at the least little thing, because it is too full. So we have to deal with the emotions as they occur, even though this is hard for most people to do. The one thing that's makes us hold negative emotions is that we don't think the person or people who have given us those negative emotions should have the angry feelings that we attach to them. We sometimes feel guilty about giving those people an understanding of how we feel and so we hide them. This is what I call short term gain for long term pain, we may feel ok to start with but as more and more negative feelings appear then the cooker gets fuller and it will explode, usually in the most inappropriate ways or time.

The way to release those emotions in a safe way is to deal with them as they appear, by you and in a way that does not involve other people seeing them or knowing about them. If you allow other people to see or know your inner most thoughts and feelings then you do not know how they will treat them, with respect, ridicule them, share them with others and or use them against you.

So the way I suggest my Clients do this is to write letters, letters that will never be sent or read by anyone else, they are safe and secure. The letters have a structure that you must follow for them to work most effectively.
- Always write the letters by hand if you cannot do this then you could speak them into a tape recorder, the old fashioned ones with a magnetic tape, or draw them.
- The first thing that you have to do is address the letter to a singularity, a one. It does not have to be a person it could be a feeling, a concept, an organisation, a part of your body, behaviour or it can be a person. If you were writing a letter to loss as a concept for example and a person who had died was brought into the letter then you would have a vastly different reaction of feeling to a concept than you would have to a person. If this did happen then have a piece of paper at the side of you and make a list of other things you would write to.
- The next thing is that you have to write how you feel about what or who you are writing to, not necessarily what happened but how you feel about what happened, as we are trying to expel the feelings from you.
- The last thing is that you have to instantly destroy the letter in any way that is appropriate, do not read it or spell check it destroy it as soon as you have finished it.

- If you were writing it at night and you were tired and thought you would finish it in the morning, then no destroy the one you are writing do another letter in the morning and destroy that one as well completely.

Write as many letters as you like you will know when you have externalised all the negative feelings about the one when you can think of it or them and it does not affect you at all. Write often and never let your pressure cooker build up.

How we deal with emotions

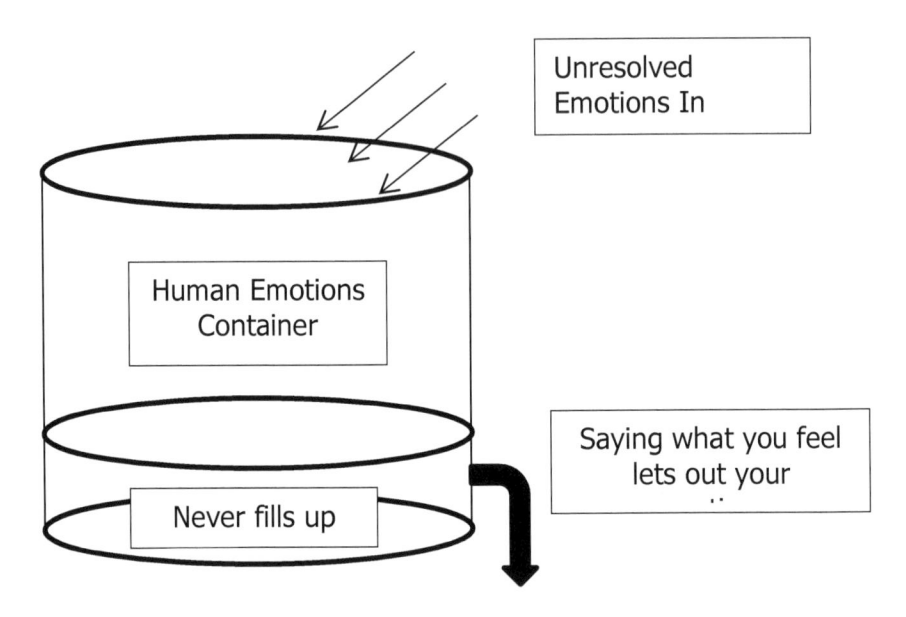

Unresolved Emotions In

Human Emotions Container

Never fills up

Saying what you feel lets out your ..

If you always say what you feel to people then your container never fills up and you will be able to cope with life more easily. If you don't say what you feel then you will always have an underlying aspect of unresolved emotions, those then will try to escape in your encounters with other humans, normally with the closest person to you. This creates resentment and arguments, try to let your feelings out never keep them in.

Keeping them in destroys letting them out solves

The Route away from Depression

This is for people suffering from depression and for people who are trying to help people who are suffering from depression. My aim is to give you an understanding of what depression is and give you the tools and ways to cope with and deal with it. First of all I would like to give you my understanding of what depression is and the dynamics it creates in people. Depression is a process and a way that human beings cope with trauma and not being able to adjust to the outside world. It stems from some aspect of feeling or perceiving that we are out of control and being depressed is a way that we can take control. This may be a strange way to look at it, but when we are depressed then we want only to be responsible for ourselves, we move away from others, sometimes people close to us that really care for us. We cannot be responsible for other people s feelings or life expectancies so we isolate ourselves and start to detach from the world as we know it and build our own little bubble or pit, safe place. We can call this place lots of different names, but in essence it is a safe place which we and only we are able to be in. We feel safe and protected being in our own little space as it gets smaller and smaller, tighter and tighter, pushing others away.

We will withdraw from society, work, responsibilities in fact anything which we feel wants something from us, we are not able to give anymore and this can lead to us hiding in our homes and sometimes even in our own rooms, not even being able to get out of bed, is a common thing, not a nice thing but a common thing.

When I work with people experiencing depression the first thing is to get them to understand that this a normal aspect of being a human being, I try to remove the stigma that society places on the depressed state of mind. Medicine can help people to cope with this state but it will, in my opinion, only ever allow them to function not to move completely back from their depressed state and they will normally never find the complete route back from being depressed without other outside help, called talking therapies, from people like myself a Counsellor. People who have people they love always ask me how can I help them to pull themselves together, they never can because they are part of the problem, in a round a bout way. People who are depressed will only see friend's family's interventions as more pressure so will withdraw even more, if others who are part of their world try to help. Counsellors can help because they are not part of the client's world they are not involved or have any part to play in there every day life. There is no responsibility on the client's part with the Counsellor.

The first rule of any help is we can only help if the person suffering believes A) they need help and B) they take responsibility for their position and want to come back from this place they are in. If they have no understanding of this place they are in then they will not see it as a problem and thus not need to be or do anything else.

Sometimes people can live with being depressed for a long period of time before they breakdown, they will never see themselves as depressed, but the drip, drip, effect will slowly build up and then it will be just one more thing that puts them over the edge, which is usually a shock for the people around them, as they will normally see that person as always coping, taking huge responsibility for others, being the one that always wants everything just so or has high standards that can't be achieved, this is usually a common trait of people more prone to depression.

In order to understand the process of coming back from this place I will use an example of a person who cannot get out of the house, they have had a long period of depression and that has made them unable to interact with the outside world, because the outside world is so scary, as anything could happen if they step outside their door, they would be out of control in that external environment.

The first rule as I said is to help them understand that this is a natural thing to happen, which it is.

The next step is to understand why they are here in the first place, what brought them down this path, it will usually stem from some out of control or a perceived out of control situation, loss or rejection, whether perceived or real it doesn't matter, can be an influencing factor.
When this has been explored then we have to find something they would like to change in their life, something they would want to take control of, this should initially be a small thing, as if you try to change big things straight away they will always fail, and failure supports there view they are not worthy or can't change anything. It might be for example, someone who is confined to the house just opening the post, anything that comes through the door will normally be scary, it's interacting or coming into their safe world, disrupting there routine etc.
If this was the case then I would set up a plan, a structure to achieve this task.
I would break it down into even smaller steps, say watching the post come through the door maybe first, touching one letter the second, holding it for a small amount of time the third, keeping hold of it fourth, taking it into their room could be fifth, opening it could be sixth, dealing with it could be seventh etc. etc., you get the idea. I would then break those steps down into even smaller ones.

Watching the post is broken down into thinking about it first, not even seeing it just thinking about seeing it.

When we think about it we would then record in a book what our stress or anxiety level is on a scale of 1 to 10, we do this in order to see our reactions external to our minds, as the mind or thought cannot be trusted initially, most people who are depressed find it very hard to contain or hold a thought, as even thoughts have responsibility.

When we have thought about it and the anxious level has reduced to under 5, this may take a few days in itself and be a very tiring process, but we reward the effort as a step forward, which it is, then when this step has been scored under 5 we would move on to the next step. Touching the letter recording our anxiety level until it reduces to fewer than 5 and so on. If we reach a state of over anxious feelings once we have achieved a step, if say we have been ok touching the post and we are at a level of 4 and then for some reason our anxiety level just increases dramatically we can retreat 1 step only, no more, as we have already achieved that step and not been anxious about it. If you retreat more than 1 step you increase the failure feeling and this will take you back to the start.
It's a bit like climbing a hill and losing your footing then starting to slide down the hill; if you don't dig your heels in then the momentum will carry you down the hill faster and faster, ending up in a heap at the bottom.

Moving from one step to another and recording it as you go, so you can look back on your achievements, shows you can change, you can move forward, taking responsibility of your world and bringing you back down that route from the path of depression. You may then look at taking control of getting dressed, again breaking it down into smaller steps thinking about it first recording it then doing it and recording it.

Then to moving forward constructing a programme of being able to go out of the door, and so on, till you take full control of your life again. Becoming depressed is a process so it make's sense that coming back is a process also.

Another tool is to record a Mood Diary, this helps us to look back again on what has happened in reality not in our head.

A Mood Diary is a book which records our mood during the day. You enter your mood first thing in a morning again on a scale of one to ten and at then also at the end of the day before you go to bed. During the day if you mood significantly changes you also record that and what is going on for your mood to change, this can give you an awareness of the triggers to your individual depression factors, what incidences change your mood and why. Again this mood diary process records your progress, bearing in mind Rome was not built in a day so it will take some time to change your mood significantly.

Also the three things we need to help change our mood is.

1 Exercise first thing in a morning a short walk will be suffice of maybe 10 minutes or 5 to start with, if 10 is too much, again increasing and recording it day to day.
2 Have a healthy diet, don't snack or eat processed foods and eat regularly.
3 Try to socialise even if you don't talk to people nod to them, but mix with people in a social interaction.

If you plan your strategy and do all these things then you will change your mood and your depressive state and live a healthier life and a more interactive life also.

Why people use put downs and ways to stop it

Why people use put downs and ways to stop it

You know the feeling being targeted and put down by someone, made to feel isolated and bullied. Why do people do that to others, well what I am about to share may shock you, but with my personal experience and professional awareness I hope I can give you a different view of this and a new way of reacting to it.
Humans put other humans down, due in my experience, to one of two factors which are both connected. The first is that they are jealous of the person they are putting down and the second is that they would like to be them in some way of another. Both these aspects are connected due to an insecure base on the person who is doing the putting down or bullying. This may surprise you and another surprise might be that you are in the power position, they need you to increase their security, you do not need them due to the fact that you are strong and secure, and hence the reason they put you down. If you can see the situation in this way it gives you the power and not be the victim, covered more fully in other areas of this site, in how to regain your power and change your perception.

The bully can only exist when they have the people they are bullying without you they're on their own and then they don't have the power or can even exist. If you can see it from this perspective then you can change the situation not being them doing it to you but they need you to do it.

I have been through this process in real life through my school years, details of which I will not bore you with, suffice to say that it followed the path of which most people find themselves in being bullied. One day it became so bad that I did not want to live and I came to a choice, which seemed to become so clear. Do I allow him to ruin my life or do I take control, a pivotal moment, and in that moment my desire to help others was born, people like me who had been targeted or was different and subjected to bullying. I saw my power in my difference I did not need to be connected to anyone, or to be cool, or to be part of the group, I revelled in my ability to be separate and not needing to be connected. Once I saw that this was a way to be free, and me, then the bullying took a different role I saw that what the person bullying me wanted was my reaction, my emotional pain.

I turned the corner and grew in self-esteem and confidence and became strong and turned my back on them, refusing to give them that reaction. This experience gave me so much power that I physically grew as well, I'm not sure if this physical aspect of growth was connected or just a coincidence.

If you can realise that they need you and you don't need them then you can change the process and take your strength.

If someone starts to put you down then a way to change that destructive process is to make them realise that they are insecure and that you care about them and that you can be with them, connect with them, without this destructive aspect. You can help them to be secure without it having to resort to this non helpful approach which will produce a win win approach.

If for example a person at work was being bullied by their boss or manager then they can approach that Manager, on a one on one basis not with others around, and ask them why it was that they felt so insecure with them, if it was that they thought that you wanted their job, a usual reason for work place bullying that others are better than the bully, then make them aware that you don't want to be them or have their job, you just want to get on with your life in peace. If that cannot happen then you will have to take this further, not that you want to do that but they would give you no choice by their actions, making them own it and be responsible for this action.

Using symbolism instead of words to communicate our feelings

We as humans sometimes find it hard to say what we feel so we will use symbolism to say it instead. Some of our quirkiest behaviour is in fact ways of us creating a dialogue with actions, which might sound far-fetched but has a base in the reality of the work I do and the situations I have worked with. When I have conversations with Clients about people's behaviours, that they connect with and our work is a part of. I look at not what they are doing but why they are doing it, a concept which is much more fully explored on the site. If we concentrate on what they're behaviour is resulting in, usually disharmony and conflict, then we lose the understanding and as such were unable to bring about a resolution to the problem. If we are feeling insecure then we react in order to create security for ourselves that might result in us over reaching things or creating a bigger process than need be.

An example of this could be in the argument process and we feel we are losing the argument we will normally increase the pressure by brining other people into the argument with statements like "Well so and so thinks the same as me"

This increase in numbers is rarely helpful but gives us an impression of being more secure as its not only us that sees it this way.

Another example might be that a person who feels insecure in their home could create disharmony by insisting they have some of them in the room leaving untidy behaviour processes, possible something that is theirs damaging something that is someone else's or overshadowing it, putting it on top of or being bigger than it.

In language structures we can, if feeling insecure, build the story using more and more intricate details or metaphors to explain things in the story. In this process we can lose the message in the detail and this can be really unhelpful in understanding the other person's needs or requirements.

If this happens I usually ask people to reduce their input and stay on point, saying less is sometimes more. I use my skills to reinterpret the message condensing the story to reveal the meaning and help them to regain their secure base so that they do not have to produce this symbolist reaction in the first place.

In understanding the why you can solve it understanding the what never will.

Offerings not Statements

When trying to communicate effectively it's very important that the style of communication you use helps you to open up the dialogue between the parties and to bring either more clarity or a resolution to the reason for having the communication. The style of communication that will help you to do this is what I would call offerings. Offerings are open question which elicit opportunities to grow the conversation bring clarity and a resolution.
An example of offering would be saying
"How do you think you are going to make that happen?" This offering gives people the opportunity to have a say in the dialogue and the process, it is an open question as more dialogue will come from it and start an exploration process.
A statement would be
"If I was you I would do this" This statement gives no opportunity for exploration it gives the receiving person no input and can either stop the conversation or lead to an argument, as the other person could feel they are being told, as they are, and then they might take exception to being told thus responding with frustration and possibly anger, this is a closed question.

An offering gives the person a choice and also responsibility for their part in the conversation and also in the outcome of the conversation, whatever that might be.

If you linked this process to the theory of TA "Transactional Analysis" then the offerings would be given to child position in order to enable them, if they accepted the offerings, to move them to an adult position. As in order to move to the Adult the Child needs to be given and to take responsibility for the process, whatever that might be. It is thought that Adult to Adult conversations are best and achieve the best results.

So in conclusion offerings are openings for Adult conversation and positive engagements whilst Statements are closings and result in negative dialogue.

Time together and apart, getting the right balance, for a healthy relationship

In this month of February it's normal for us to connect more to our partners and loved ones. We send cards go out and possibly treat them with gifts or thoughts. It also surprises me that we create lives which are so busy that we sometimes put the most important relationship, on a back burner for the rest of the year, so to speak. It's as though we do not try with these closest relationships because they should know we care about them and that we love them, we don't need to tell them in our words and actions because it should be a given.

Many of the people I see, who have been in relationships which have broken down, find that they put their primary relationship second to all other relationships that they have. I firmly believe that the primary relationship is as important as any other relationship they have, if not more important, it is the glue that holds all other family relationships together. The most informed awareness we have about healthy relationships tells us that we have to have connections with all the people we love and care about but also we have to have exclusive quality time just as the couple as well.

This life nowadays is so frantic and stressful and time away from work and job roles gets less and less, as we look to provide more and more for our families and life. When I talk to people who are trying to re-connect relationships I always find that they have stopped or vastly reduced spending quality time together or that they spend too much time together in each other's lives both can be a negative process. It seems that the best balance is having exclusive time together, separate time on hobbies or other social interactions as well as time with all the other roles we have whether that is work, families or other connections. Getting this balance right is very hard to do but has to happen in a way that keeps all connections healthy and interconnected.

One way to do this with your primary relationship is to book time together, a fuller understanding of how to do this can be found on this site, otherwise other connections become more important, we normally look to provide others needs to the detriment of our own.

This staged managed process for some couples can be seen as controlling and not impulsive, but as I have said usually if it's not given this structure then sometimes it just does not happen, which definitely is not helpful in bringing people together.

The reason why time apart is also important is that it helps to bring in new conversations and new perspectives on life; it can recharge our batteries so to speak.

This separateness can also help to forge our individual identity and help us to grow as people, for the benefit of the relationship, as if we are more fulfilled then we will be happier and more content with our lives. This aspect is usually an important feature of Women or Men who have just become Mums or Dads as in the first years of our new parental role people describe us as our children's name Mum or Dad, oh its D******* Mum or Dad, we lose our individual identity which can be real problem for people who are just in the role of Parent and have no other role or external connection.

Balance your time and continually look to see if it fits your needs and makes you happy, if not then re-balance, with the input of the other people close to you, so they know the reason that you are doing it and that they will benefit from it. If couples who are in distress, due to not spending enough quality time together, asked the people close to them if they can look after the children so they can spend some quality time together, then I have never found those people refuse and say they would not want to do that. When people say to me in the counselling room that they cannot find time for them I usually say but you can and have by being here with me. This reality is something which sometimes creates a shock in the room but cannot be argued with.

See your relationship as important as any other relationship you have and give it the same respect it will help you have a healthy and happy relationship for many years to come.

Is your Relationship in need of help?

10 questions to check your relationships health and quality, in no particular order of importance or criticality:

Do you find that you are quibbling over things which seem unimportant?

Are you spending less quality time together as a couple?

Do you feel apprehensive about going home?

Do you feel listened to by your partner?

Are you spending less time sexually connected than you think you used to be?

Are small things getting on your nerves?

Do you spend more time away from home than you used to?

Are you engaging and communicating with other people things you should be talking to your partner about?

Are you having thoughts of hurting or harming yourself or others?

Are you using deflective behaviours like drink or drugs in order not to be in the real world?

If you can answer yes to three or more of these statements then you may need to check your relationships health and quality and start to rebuild it looking at the chapter re-making connection. If you can answer yes to six or more of the statements then you are in the process of a relationship breakdown and may need to seek expert help to bring it back from the brink of collapse.

Process to change

Moving forward is a process but one in which the person wishing to move is aware of the reasons for being unable to release the past. In moving forward we have to take our responsibility in why we are where we are. This taking responsibility in some ways stops us being the victim, a non-responsible person. In doing this taking of responsibility for your position we release the chains of the past, which bind us and stops us moving on. Next we have to understand where we want to move to, this process is classed as the plan. We have to initially use a plan in order to see forward momentum as how can we know if we have moved if we cannot measure it. The plan then needs to be broken down into as small steps as you can in order for it to be achieved. Large steps are unlikely to initially achieve goals just despondences when you don't get there, meaning you are less likely to try in the future. This constant I'm going to process but never does is usually because we perceive it arduous a task or there's no point. Our perception is our reality but often not the actual reality; we have to be aware of this viewpoint as it can inhibit us from moving forward in a constructive way. Sometimes non movement is because we don't feel we deserve it, the goal, we self-sabotage the process, put a spanner in the works type of thing or we believe we will never amount to anything so what is the point in trying.

Using deflective behaviours

We use lots of ways to help us not to have to face things that are hard for us to do so I call this using deflective behaviours. These behaviours can be many and very varied dependant on how we see an escape opportunity. Usually this will be to escape from feelings but not always, as sometimes we try to escape from reality and responsibility. If you need to understand whether behaviour is indeed deflective then it will be that the person using that behaviour will not get the high or the effect they wanted to gain from it. An example would be if someone shopped to enable their deflection process they would have lots of things but will not find fulfilment in having them after buying each one they will not use it or hide it away from sight, a way of hiding from sight their emotions. We as loved ones and as a society sometimes focus on the deflection behaviour, trying to stop it or make them feel bad about doing it. This rarely helps and usually results in them stopping that behaviour but finding another one equally as destructive, it just moves and sometimes even multiplies the acting out of both behaviours instead of just the original one. The hardest thing for us to face when we have someone who is exhibiting this form of deflection is that we are a part of their pain and suffering, which is why we concentrate on the behaviour, the what, instead of the reason for it, the why.

How many of us have, after going through some emotional pain, have gone out and done something totally against our normal behaviour, a release but then after we have returned to normality regretted it and the emotional pain is still there which we have to still deal with. These deflective behaviours then can if used constantly become habit forming and can result in an ongoing deflective process which we will always turn to, after we have encountered something emotional that we cannot deal with, or even if we perceive it will be happening in the future.

Our perception is our reality even if it does not sense to anyone else.

Once we succumb to this process then we find ourselves in a circular process that initially helps us to deal with life but then becomes more and more of our life. There is some research about Nature, part of us, and Nurture, part of what we have been shown or told which comes into this process, such as addictions and self-destructive behaviours.

In my professional world and my experience we react to things which then make things happen, so nothing can be in isolation, everything is a reaction to something else, even if we do not understand it, as it could be a sub conscious process instead of a conscious decision.

Try to understand why you are doing what you are doing and then see if that satisfies you or if it leaves you with feelings of dissatisfaction, if the latter then you need to change it or come to understand why you do it, if the former then that might be helpful.

Immediacy

When working with immediacy it is most important that you have a good therapeutic bond with the Client and that it is strong enough to cope with challenge. I would refer you back to the Intuitive process section to help you with engaging and producing strong therapeutic bonds with Clients. Once you are aware that you have this good working bond then I would suggest that you set up as part of the contract with an understanding that you will use immediacy if appropriate when working with the Client.
Why is using immediacy so important?
The use of immediacy not only helps the Client or Clients to understand what is happening in the moment but it also gives them an insight into how they can change what they do to have a better outcome. An example of this would be a partner of a couple in the room, one partner who is engaging in communication with the other is not being assertive but being verbally abusive by their body language, aggressively pointing their finger, by the blaming words they are using. If you allow the process to develop then the other person they are engaging with may withdraw or may engage more forcibly and an argument may ensue. If you interrupt the process, before the communication becomes destructive, and engage with the person talking with immediacy then they can see what they are doing.

Being abusive, and that they can change their presentation, with intervention, to achieve a better outcome. In the example above I would always confer with the other partner who is being verbally abused whether they are feeling as I am thinking they are feeling, I would never assume what I am perceiving is the reality, as I would then be abusing the Client's.

What is the positive outcome of using immediacy?
In the example given by interrupting the process you will have given the abuser the option of change and the abused someone who can support them in how they are feeling. This can make a whole lot of difference to the Client's as most of the people I see really want to change to be different and anything we as Therapists can do to help that will give great rewards to them and us. The abuser will have a choice to change and realise what they are doing and the effect that it is having on their relationship. This will ultimately help the abused person to see that their partner cares enough about them to alter their ways and that the feelings they were having were not wrong to have.

This will undoubtedly have a positive influence on both how they communicate and interact, the building blocks of any good relationship and the only way to alter and change the negative impacts of life, positive and respectful talking helps the healing.

My way of working may not be for all therapists but the focus of how I work relies on, if it helps the Client then my job is to change what I do to help them to not need me. I work with an evolving integrative style and change how I present my work based on the Client's needs if my style is not appropriate then I ask them to tell me, not to just disengage, and I will try to alter my style to fit the Client's requirements.

Having hard conversations

The first thing to realise is that people will not be open to this conversation if they feel that they have to lose face by having it, so the conversation needs to be discussed one to one not in a group.

The second phase is to let them know the way you feel, without the possibility of conflict, the way to do this is for you to own the conversation; it's always about you and your feelings never about what has happened.

The third phase is to tell them you want a closer connection with them in some way, normally the other party wants this also so it's a win win.

The fourth phase is to plant the responsibility of getting there firmly on their shoulders, saying it cannot be achieved without them, this will give them the assumption of power and that they are in charge of the process.
Really difficult conversations have been had with this formula and achieved success.

Finally

"Take control and have the life you want not the one you or others think you deserve"